Especially for
ATHLETES

SHAD MARTIN **&** DUSTIN SMITH

Especially for
ATHLETES

LEADERSHIP ON AND OFF THE FIELD

FOREWORD BY **TY DETMER**
HEISMAN TROPHY WINNER

ISBN 13: 978-1-4621-1201-2

Published by CFI, an imprint of Cedar Fort, Inc., 2373 W. 700 S., Springville, UT 84663
Distributed by Cedar Fort, Inc., www.cedarfort.com

LIBRARY OF CONGRESS CATALOGING-IN-PUBLICATION DATA

Martin, Shad, 1976- author.
Especially for athletes : leadership on and off the field / Shad Martin and Dustin Smith.
    pages cm
ISBN 978-1-4621-1201-2 (alk. paper)
1. Athletes--Life skills guides. 2. Athletics--Sociological aspects. 3. Work ethic. 4. Leadership. I. Smith, Dustin, 1977- author. II. Title.

GV706.55.M37 2013
306.483--dc23

                        2013002139

Cover design by Shawnda T. Craig
Cover design © 2013 Lyle Mortimer
Edited and typeset by Emily S. Chambers

Printed in the United States of America

10 9 8 7 6 5 4 3 2 1

CONTENTS

FOREWORD

I wholeheartedly agree with the principles taught in *Especially for Athletes*. Over the last several years, I have heard the authors explain to young athletes many of the principles from this book, and I believe them to be true. I have also come to know the authors on a personal level as well as a professional level, and I appreciate the values they share with so many of our youth. The message of the book is important to everyone, but it is especially important to athletes and the parents of athletes because of the opportunities and the attention that athletes receive while playing sports. The authors refer to this attention as the "sportlight." The book explains how athletes can use their time in the "sportlight" to not only grow themselves but also to lift and bless those around them. Dustin and Shad do a terrific job at teaching this message.

You have a lot of responsibility in being athletes not only to your team but also to the others you may influence. I have been fortunate to be in a position to influence others through athletics and have personally seen the impact athletes can have both for the positive and the negative. In this age of sports, we sometimes get caught up in getting ahead instead of living in the moment and taking the time to influence others in a positive way. We are seeing too many athletes today who take advantage of the system and have a "me first" attitude only to later regret their actions and, in too many cases, ruin their reputation and crush others' opinion of them.

I have had times in my personal life when I have been knocked down and have had to dust myself off and go back to work to be better the next time around, and like the book explains, I had to "do the work" with my "eyes up." That is a message every young athlete should read and try to follow.

After retiring from the NFL, and through the benefits of social media, I have been able to reconnect with a lot of people and have heard from great fans and old friends. The message I hear that I'm most proud of are those that people share letting me know that they appreciate the friend I was back in high school, and, despite my winning the Heisman Trophy and my playing in the NFL, that I treated them kindly. I have played with some guys over the years that turned people away when asked for an autograph, and it was always disappointing to see the looks on kids' faces as they walked away empty handed. Some guys proclaimed that they weren't a role model, or that they didn't sign up for that responsibility, but I believe when you sign up to play a sport, that responsibility comes with the commitment to play. In the book it is referred to as the "sportlight" and "seeking to bless, not to impress."

If you follow the five principles in this book, I know that you will be able to be a positive influence on your team, in your family, and in your community. I can't think of a better book for young athletes to be able to use to help relate athletics to life. Use that "sportlight" to be a great person and a great athlete and influence others for good. *Especially for Athletes* and the programs and events being organized around its principles will help you in that quest.

—**Ty Detmer**

ESPECIALLY FOR PARENTS

We hope that this book facilitates many wonderful discussions between you and your young athletes. We know that some of the greatest life lessons we have learned came after ball games on the car ride home with our parents. There is something special about that time. Though we wrote this book to young athletes, we hope that some parents read it too and that the hundreds of hours we spent refining these words and concepts can help you to teach and reach your children during these special moments.

There are times in teenagers' lives when they are more ready to learn than others. We believe that sports create many of those moments. God bless you as you strive to help your children learn the valuable, life-changing lessons that can come from playing sports. We hope that you can have the effect on your children that our parents had on us.

Introduction

IT'S MORE THAN JUST A GAME

While traveling around the country speaking with hundreds of different youth groups, we began to realize that a few principles seemed especially relevant to young athletes. Being an athlete will bring with it many opportunities for you to learn invaluable lessons and do good to those around you. A phrase that we like to use is called the "sportlight." This refers to the extra attention and opportunity afforded you at school and in the community because you are an athlete. How can you use this opportunity in the "sportlight" to its fullest? That is what this book will discuss. While the principles in this book are applicable to everyone, we have designed these principles to be especially for athletes, hence the title.

Maybe we should start by telling you what this book is not. It is not a "rah rah, you can do anything you put your mind to" book. It is also not merely a collection of fun or inspiring stories that a young sports enthusiast would enjoy reading. Those things are wonderful, but this book is designed to be more than that. We have often heard people say, "It's just a game!" It is our deep belief that sports can be so much more than a just a game. They are a training ground for life. This book invites you to take a deeper look at the opportunities God has given you to grow through participation in athletics.

1

When approached properly, athletics can be a vehicle to learning some of the most important lessons in life. The principles that will make you a great athlete are the same principles that will make you a great student, parent, spouse, employee, and servant of the Lord. *Sports* give you an avenue to *master* these principles; *life* gives you the chance to *apply* them. In this book, we hope to introduce you to five principles that will help you become the best athlete you can be. We will then discuss how those same principles can be applied to other areas of your life so that you can become all that God intended for you to become. The game itself is just that—a game, meaning it's not life or death. But the lessons we learn from the game can be life changing.

The five principles we will discuss in this book are

Do the Work
Compete without Contempt
Seek To Bless, Not To Impress
First Things First
Strive To Be *Your* Best, Not *The* Best

These five principles are applicable to everyone—to stars of teams and to supporting players. They are applicable to junior high, high school, college, and professional athletes. Both of us have played sports all of our lives, including college baseball together, and we have taught and coached thousands of youth over the last decade. As we look back at the lessons we have learned from our involvement in sports, we have realized how big of an impact those lessons have had on our lives. Our goal is to help you recognize at an earlier age how big of an impact these principles can have upon your life. Focused concentration on these five principles will increase the positive impact that sports can have on your personal development.

At the heart of these five principles will be two phrases.

These phrases are woven throughout each chapter, so we wanted to briefly introduce them here so you would be familiar with them and understand what we mean by them. We encourage you to have these two phrases in the back of your mind as you read each chapter because they are a short summation of the overarching message we hope you will take from this book.

Phrase One: "Do the Work"

Do the work. What good is knowledge unless it is applied? Reading this book without doing what is suggested would be like watching an exercise DVD on the couch and wondering why you're not getting stronger. The first chapter is dedicated to this phrase, but you will quickly recognize that mastering every principle talked about in this book will require you to "do the work." "Do the work" means to take action, to go and do, and to start your journey toward reaching your goals.

Phrase Two: "Eyes Up"

Eyes up. This means that you look vertically instead of horizontally for your feedback. In other words, you have an "eyes up" attitude looking to God for his approval and guidance instead of taking your cues from the world and responding to its ever-shifting opinions. When times get tough, "eyes up"—you look to God for comfort and perspective instead of to the world and its discouraging feedback. When you have success, "eyes up"—you look to God in gratitude instead of to the world for praise or attention. In short, you live your life with your eyes up looking for feedback from heaven. It also means you don't hang your head in discouragement when the road to your achievements becomes difficult. You keep your eyes up and focused on your goal.

These two phrases work in harmony with each other. Having your *eyes up* will help you obtain the right *direction*; *doing the work* will help you reach your *destination*.

3

We hope that at the end of this book, you will be better able to see that your participation in athletics can be much more than just playing a game. It is mission prep, job prep, marriage prep, and parenthood prep. It is preparation for life.

The book is organized in such a way that you will be challenged to think about how you are doing with each of the principles discussed. Throughout each chapter we will have what we call "twenty-second time-outs." They will look like this:

Twenty-Second Time-Out

What do you think we mean when we say "Sports are more than just a game"?

_____

_____

_____

_____

_____

_____

_____

_____

_____

_____

_____

_____

_____

We encourage you to think deeply about the questions with an "eyes up" attitude, and to "do the work" by writing down your thoughts and impressions about how the principles discussed specifically apply to your life. You may be tempted to just get through this book and to skip these mental exercises. The point is not to get through this book but to let the principles in this book pass through you and become part of your life. The thoughts and impressions that you will write down during these twenty-second time-outs will be the most important words written on these pages when you are all done reading it.

At the end of each chapter will also be a "do the work" workout page. This is where you will look over what you have written throughout the chapter and make specific goals to "do the work" in that area of your sports and personal life. We encourage you to really make an effort to "do the work." This will be most effective when you make what are called SMART goals. SMART is an acronym. SMART goals are goals that are Specific, Measurable, Attainable, Results oriented, and Time framed.

Here is an example of a goal that is not SMART:
I will get stronger.

Here is what a SMART goal looks like:
I will lift four times each week for the whole summer, keeping track of my weight and reps, and try to increase my weight or reps each week.

Do you see the difference between the two goals and why the second goal would be so much more effective? The second goal is Specific, you can Measure whether or not you are accomplishing it, it is Attainable, meaning it is realistically something you could accomplish if you were willing to do the work, it is Results oriented, meaning that it is focused on something you want to achieve, and it is Time framed, which means you can look back at the end of the summer and see if you accomplished it.

Like we mentioned above, you may also be tempted to skip the "do the work" workout pages. Please do not do that. As with anything, you do not grow from hearing or watching or reading; you grow from *doing*.

We pray that the principles within this book will be a blessing to you. We know that they have been to us. By applying these principles to your life, sports can become more than "just a game." They can be a tutor and help you develop the skills necessary to have a successful life. They can shape your life. Now let's go do the work with an eyes up attitude!

Chapter 1

DO THE WORK

Pregame Pep Talk

"I have been impressed with the urgency of doing.
Knowing is not enough; we must apply.
Being willing is not enough; we must do."
—Leonardo da Vinci

"Without ambition one starts nothing.
Without work one finishes nothing.
The prize will not be sent to you. You have to win it."
—Ralph Waldo Emerson

"I firmly believe that any man's finest hour, the greatest
fulfillment of all that he holds dear, is the moment
when he has worked his heart out in a good cause and lies
exhausted on the field of battle—victorious."
—Vince Lombardi

"The heights by great men reached and kept,
Were not attained by sudden flight.
But they, while their companions slept
Were toiling upward in the night."
—Henry Wadsworth Longfellow

One of the great blessings that comes from playing sports is the opportunity to learn to work. In a world where many young people are not learning this valuable lesson, you have the chance to learn it and reap the blessings from it. Playing sports provides you the occasion to push yourself and find out what you are really made of. Because you play sports, you are blessed with coaches that push you and help you discover abilities and energies that you may have never discovered otherwise. It is no accident that this is the first of the five principles covered in this book, for without this principle the others won't matter much either. Why? Because these are not easy quick-fix principles. Mastering each will require work on your part. You are probably going to have successes and failures with each one, and you are going to have to do the work to accomplish them and reap the blessings.

What Does "Do the Work" Mean?

You may think that to "do the work" means to simply go through the motions and mandatory drills required of you to be on the team. That is doing the bare minimum, not doing the work, at least not the way that *we* define doing the work. We love the word "extraordinary." Look at that word closely. It's a combination of the words "extra" and "ordinary." Simply going through the motions is what an "ordinary" athlete would do. We want you to think about being "extra-ordinary," or in others words, we want you to think about how you can go beyond the bare minimum. To really do the work you must set lofty goals and then be steady, energetic, passionate, and determined, with your "eyes up" continually focused on accomplishing them.

Learning to Do the Work Brings Independence

When we use the phrase "do the work," we view it as a very personal thing. It is easy to pretend to work hard, to pretend to "leave it all on the field." You can contort your face or strain your muscles in such a way that those around you think you are giving it your all and leaving it all on the field. When all is said and done, only you and God will really know whether you gave your full effort or not. Learning to do the work on your own brings independence. How? Some players make great strides when they have a coach who demands a lot of them but then digress when they have a coach on the opposite end of the scale who does not demand as much or when they are in the off season and a coach is not allowed to have as much contact with them. It is an awesome thing to learn to grow regardless of your circumstances. It is a wonderful thing to set a personal goal and then do the work necessary to accomplish it. That feeling of conquering the goal you set out to conquer will become contagious, and you and those around you will want to feel it again and again. What a great experience that is! That contagious feeling of accomplishment will lead you to become a self-motivated person who seeks to be your very best at everything you do and someone who will not settle for being mediocre, average, or ordinary. That is how champions become champions. Average athletes put forth ordinary effort. Those who become great put forth extraordinary effort.

Twenty-Second Time-Out

What goal have you set and then worked toward accomplishing with an extra-ordinary effort? How did it feel?

_____

_____

_____

_____

_____

_____

_____

_____

_____

_____

_____

Stars and "Benchwarmers" Need to Work

It is important that you understand at a young age that to be your best as an athlete—and in all the other areas of your life—nothing worth much will ever come to you without you working for it. Champions must earn that title, and it is earned as much, if not more, before the game than during it. Your efforts early in the morning while others sleep, or on the days you don't "have to practice" but choose to do so anyway, are what will help you become an extraordinary athlete. During the off-season, most can't wait to get away from the grind of workouts. Champions, on the other hand, can't wait to get back to work because they understand the title of "champion" must be earned and that good old-fashioned sweat and hard work is the price to be paid.

This principle is equally applicable to all athletes, whether you are currently the star of the team or a "benchwarmer." Far too often physically gifted young men and woman do not reach their full potential as athletes because they rely too much on natural ability and believe that those they are able to outperform now will never improve. They act as though being the best is something they have the right to and that they can simply wake up and head to the field or court and dominate because they have done so in the past. To those of you who are fortunate enough to be on top of the athletic mountain now, you must realize that without the focus and discipline necessary to do the work, you will find yourself on the bottom looking up at someone who outworked you.

Now for you "benchwarmers"—those of you who feel like you are on the bottom looking up to those who are more athletically gifted you—you only have one hope: do the work. There is not a fairy godmother who is going to come and wave her magic wand and turn you into an extraordinary athlete. If you do not have extraordinary talent you must have extra-extraordinary work ethic. No one is going to do that for you. You must choose to do the work.

Famous football coach Vince Lombardi once said, "The dictionary is the only place that success comes before work. Hard work is the price we must pay for success. I think you can accomplish anything if you're willing to pay the price" (http://www.leadership-with-you.com/vince-lombardi-leadership.html).

Examples of Those Who Have Done the Work

There are numerous stories of successful men and women who made it a consistent habit in their daily lives to *do* what was necessary in order to accomplish their goals. Some people work hard to get a position on the team, some work hard to get more playing time, but the special ones are the ones who work without a final destination. This does not mean that they do not have goals; however, they view their goals as checkpoints. Once they reach their goal, they set another. They believe that they can always get better and they consider each day as an opportunity to do so. They refuse to settle for being or becoming ordinary and never become satisfied. These people crave improvement and work to achieve it. These people become champions. They become extraordinary.

To do the work, you will sometimes need to sacrifice the comforts of today for the prizes of tomorrow. It may mean sacrificing sleep or a warm bed on a cold morning to wake up earlier and exercise. It may mean sacrificing some foods that taste good for ones that are good for you. It means sweating and pushing yourself, sacrificing the comfort and relief that would come from sitting and resting. It means sacrificing some TV and video game time so that you can go to bed in order to be rested for more important things. It means sacrificing your pride in order to look for constructive criticism from those that are there to help you improve. This all should be kept in proper balance of course, which we dedicated a whole chapter to, titled "First Things First." What we're talking about is diligently doing the work in the proper time allotted you to do so. Keeping your eyes up will allow you to know when you may have crossed that line.

Consider Kobe Bryant as an example. His accomplishments are so numerous that they could make up a book in and of themselves. Some people are his biggest fans while others dislike Kobe, but love him or hate him, there is one thing that even his worst critics should admire about him: his tenacious work ethic. In a story written about Bryant, Jay Triano, an NBA assistant coach and an assistant coach for the U.S. Olympic team, shared an experience of watching Kobe in a high school gym well after practice for the Olympic basketball team had ended. While other athletes were out on the town or at home resting, Triano saw something he described as "amazing." Kobe Bryant was in the gym doing the work. He explained it in his own words:

He's not just going through the motions when he's shooting jump shots. They're game shots, at game speed. And the repetition . . . over and over and over. Like, three-point shots. There are a lot of (NBA) guys, you'll watch them make 25 from each spot. He's like, 100, 200 from the corner every night. And you'd think he'd be done and he's going on to the next spot. And he goes back and he shoots fadeaways and he shoots 'em off the bounce. I was just like, "Holy smoke." You get tired throwing the ball back, let alone shooting it. (Dave Feschuk, "If Hard Work Counts, Kobe League Best by Far," *The Star*, Apr. 2008.)

Some players can shoot better, some jump higher, some are stronger, and some are faster than Kobe. How is it that he remained so extraordinary throughout his illustrious career? He does the work in an extraordinary way. One can only wonder how many other Kobe Bryants there are in the NBA who never became what he became because they never worked like he worked.

If you want to be an extraordinary athlete, you must give an extraordinary effort!

Twenty-Second Time-Out

Is there an area in your sports life right now that you are not "doing the work" in? What can you do to begin to do the work necessary in order to develop your talents as an athlete and reach your full potential?

_____

_____

_____

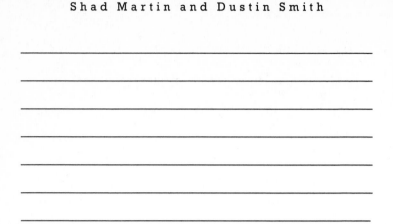

Doing the Work Requires Working through Failure

Let's not kid ourselves here. You may work for months to make the team only to get cut. You may work and work and work to make the starting lineup and not do so. You may work and sweat and bleed and still lose. Doing the work brings with it zero guarantees of accomplishing your specific goal. As a matter of fact, if you set your goals high enough, you will fail. When you fail, you may be tempted to think that all of the work and sweat and effort were in vain. At this point, many people will then quit and accept failure. Extraordinary athletes, on the other hand, treat failure as a fuel to the fiery desire within them to succeed. It motivates them to work even harder and smarter so that they can continue to get better and succeed the next time.

If you work really hard at something and then fail to achieve what you hoped to, don't accept becoming ordinary. If you let your failures drive you to work harder, you are in rare company. You are in the company of the extraordinary. Think about Michael Jordan, considered by many to be the best basketball player to ever play the game. He said the following: "I've missed more than 9,000 shots in my career. I've lost almost 300 games. Twenty-six times, I've been trusted to take the game-winning shot and missed. I've failed over and over and over again in my life. And that is why I succeed. I can accept failure, everyone fails at something. But I can't accept not trying."

How about a few off-the-field examples.

Consider world famous inventor Thomas Edison. He said, "I never did anything by accident, nor did any of my inventions come by accident; they came by work." Thomas Edison was called crazy for some of his ideas, and he failed on many occasions to produce anything useful from them, but he did not let his failures prevent him from working. His successes changed the world.

Before becoming president, Abraham Lincoln's successes were not very impressive. He could have given up, but he kept on working. Look at the time line below and think about how many times he could have stopped doing the work.

1831 – His business failed
1832 – He was defeated for legislature
1832 – He started the Black Hawk War as a captain and was demoted to a private
1833 – His second failure in business occurred
1836 – He suffered a nervous breakdown
1838 – He was defeated for Speaker of the House
1840 – He was defeated for Senate
1843 – He was defeated for Congress
1848 – He was defeated for Congress again
1855 – He was defeated for Senate again
1856 – He was defeated for Vice President
1858 – He was defeated for Senate for a third time
1860 – He was elected President of the United States of America!

Despite all of his failures, Abraham Lincoln continued to stay focused on what he wanted to become and what he wanted his country to become. Eventually his hard work paid off, and he not only became President of the United States, but in the eyes of many, he was one of the greatest presidents the county has ever had. By persevering and doing the work in spite of his failures, he quite possibly saved the county during some of the country's most difficult days.

We have all have heard of the great Walt Disney, but did you know that Walt Disney was once told he was not imaginative enough to succeed and had his first business attempt in the field of animation fail and go bankrupt? He didn't give up; he kept working. He decided to move to California with very little in his pocket. He was young and motivated and kept on working. His company suffered setbacks during its start-up. During the 1930s and the Great Depression, millions of Americans suffered and were without work, and many businesses did not survive. In the 1940s, World War II hit the country. Many of his workers were sent to war, and his Disney properties were used as storage space for military equipment. They were millions of dollars in debt; however, Disney stayed focused and kept doing the work. Most of us are familiar with his great success.

Aside from Disneyland and Disney World, Walt Disney created more than eighty films and won a record twenty-two Academy Awards. Walt Disney World Company is estimated to be worth fifty-four billion dollars. Disney once said, "I can never stand still. I must explore and experiment. I am never satisfied with my work. I resent the limitations of my own imagination."

Doing the work involves working through failure. Whether you fail or not is not always under your control; two things will always be under your control, though: your attitude and your effort. No one can control those in you but you. Those two things will enable you to do the toughest work you may ever do: to try again when you fail. There is always a risk when you give great effort that in spite of your work you will fail. Work does not guarantee success; however, quitting when you fail will guarantee failure. Famous author and speaker Leo Buscaglia said, "To try is to risk failure. But risk must be taken because the greatest hazard of life is to risk nothing. The person who risks nothing does nothing, has nothing, is nothing. He may avoid suffering and sorrow, but he simply cannot learn, feel, change, grow, live, and love."

So work to make the team, work to be a contributor to the team, work to win the championship, work to get the scholarship. You might fail. Are you willing to take that risk? More important, are you willing to take the risk of continuing to work even after you fail and fail and fail? The examples given suggest that is exactly what extraordinary people do in order to become extraordinary. They are not extraordinary because they never failed but because they didn't stop working when they failed. The question is not if life will knock you down but when. Life will knock you down. When it does, stay on your knees for a minute, then with your eyes up, ask your Father in Heaven for help, strength, and direction. Then jump back to your feet and get back to work!

Off-the-Field Applications

The scriptures tell us that during his teenage years, Jesus "increased in wisdom and stature, and in favor with God and man" (Luke 2:52). Today we might say it this way: "Jesus grew scholastically, physically, spiritually, and socially." What a great pattern for each of us to follow. Let's look at how the lessons we learn from doing the work while playing sports could be applied to these four critical areas of our lives.

Working to Grow in Wisdom (Scholastically)

The Lord has taught that "whatever principle of intelligence we attain unto in this life, it will rise with us in the resurrection" (Doctrine and Covenants 130:18–19). He then goes on to teach us that "if a person gains more knowledge and intelligence in this life through his diligence and obedience than another, he will have so much the advantage in the world to come." Notice that the Savior says we gain knowledge and intelligence through diligence. Wisdom and knowledge are not thrust upon us; we need to do the work to obtain them. Some athletes get out of balance and don't do the work scholastically. As you learn to do the work in the classroom, you will be blessed long after your playing days are over. In this scripture, when the Lord speaks of having an advantage in the "world to come," it seems as though the Lord is talking about the afterlife. We think that this could also apply to you right now in a different way. For you, "the world to come" could also mean life after high school and college. We can testify that this scripture is true in that sense as well. Those who do the work scholastically will have an advantage as they move forward. Good grades will give you an advantage as you try to get into college, and having good grades will open up more athletic opportunities. It will be easier to get a job and to support yourself and your family. It is so important to learn to do the work scholastically. If you learn to work as hard in school as you do on the field, you will have so much more the advantage in the world to come.

Dustin's Experience

My father helped me understand that I needed to be as diligent of a student as I was as an athlete at a young age. When I was a sophomore in high school, I started getting a bit out of balance with things. I was dressing varsity in three sports at a school where that was a real honor, since there were a lot of very good athletes. I had worked hard, and every day I worked to get better. I started enjoying my sports and my friends too much and didn't pay as much attention to my grades and study habits.

I didn't see much of life outside of the field and the court. My dad came to me early in my sophomore year and reminded me that in our home, I would need to maintain at least a 3.0 GPA to be able to play. I knew he was serious because the previous year, my freshman year, I lost the opportunity to play for a bit while I corrected a bad science grade. The high school required only a 2.0 to be eligible to play on the school teams, but my Dad's standard was higher. I was never concerned with falling below a 2.0, but I was not about to do one bit of work in the classroom more than necessary to get my 3.0. Once I had cleared Professor Dad's grade-point requirement, I was on to things I thought were much more important, like sports and friends. So at the disappointment of my parents and teachers, I managed to pull off 3.0s for three years. I didn't push myself; I did just enough, including begging teachers the last week of the term for extra credit and make-up assignments. The truth was, I was lazy. I was smart enough to get better grades, but I didn't want to do the work. I wanted the grades given to me. My dad wanted me to be able to play ball; he knew how much I loved it and enjoyed seeing me play, so he made it easy for me. A 3.0 did not require an extreme sacrifice on my part. I'm sure he hoped I would really focus and earn the grade I was capable of, but I did only what was needed and never really pushed myself.

When college came and I had a scholarship to play ball, all I needed was a 2.0 in order to play. What do you think my grades were during my first semester at college? I recorded a 2.3! Again, barely enough to pass the required mark, and then I was off to do other things with my time.

After one semester of school, I left for a two-year mission to be with the best people in the world (Shad may argue) in Santiago, Chile. As all young men do who go on a mission and really do the work, I changed. I grew up. My perspective on things changed and my eyes were opened to real life and real joy and sadness. When I returned, I was motivated to try to be better academically. I knew how to work. I had done so in my sports career and carried that over to my mission. I had thought about being a better student many times, but this time I was not just going to think about it, I was going to *do* it! I went back to college and did the work. I met with every teacher I had. I asked what I needed to do to get A's in their classes. I sat on the front row of class and spent many evenings when I could have been out with friends, or with my then girlfriend and later wife, Jamie, in the library studying. This is when I truly realized what doing the work in all areas of life really required. This time in my life was a major turning point. Sports had helped me learn how to do the work, I applied that lesson to my mission, and now I was applying that lesson to be the best student I could be. School was not overwhelmingly hard, but it was not as easy as throwing a ball was, and I had to really work at it. When I received my report card that semester and saw 4.0 on it, I was as proud and as happy as I had ever been. I would never settle for bad grades again, and throughout the rest of college I worked hard to be a great student. I earned it. I did the work!

Growing in Stature (Physically)

Sports help you to develop physically, and this development is important both on and off the field. Some who do not take care of their body are limited in the amount of church service they are able to render. There once was a young man that was so excited to serve a mission that he took fifteen institute courses before he left on his mission. He arrived and thrived at the MTC because all he had to do for hours a day was sit and study. He was an all-star in the MTC; however, when he hit the mission field, things changed. He really struggled and was not the missionary he dreamed he would be. Why? Because he was in such poor physical condition that he did not have the energy or stamina to do the work.

Elder L. Tom Perry said the following:

The minimum physical standard for full-time missionary service refers to a potential missionary's physical health and strength. For example, one of the questions on the missionary recommendation forms asks if you "can work 12 to 15 hours per day, walk 6 to 8 miles per day, ride a bicycle 10 to 15 miles per day, and climb stairs daily." Missionary work is hard, and full-time missionaries must be in good physical condition to serve. Raising the bar to a higher physical standard could involve further physical conditioning. (L. Tom Perry, "Raising the Bar," *Ensign*, Nov. 2007)

President Ezra Taft Benson said,

If we want to keep the Spirit, we must work. There is no greater exhilaration or satisfaction than to know, after a hard day of work, that we have done our best. I have often said that one of the greatest secrets of missionary work is work! If a missionary works, he will get the Spirit; if he gets the Spirit, he will teach by the Spirit; and if he teaches by the Spirit, he will touch the hearts of the people and he will be happy. Work, work, work—there is no satisfactory substitute, especially in missionary work. (Ezra Taft Benson, "Keys to Successful Member-Missionary Work," *Ensign*, Sept. 1990, 2)

You can learn to work in athletics and that will translate into the mission field. Think of it—the weight room, the wind sprints, the waking up early—when done correctly, it is all mission prep. Athletics are a wonderful way to prepare physically for a mission. If what President Benson said is true (and we believe that it is), if you learn to sacrifice in order to do the work physically, you have already learned one of the greatest secrets of missionary work.

Shad's Experience

I must say, when I arrived in the mission field, I was a little shocked at how hard a mission was. I was a college baseball player that had just finished the season, but waking up at 6:30 each morning, studying for a couple of hours, and then leaving the apartment at 9:30 a.m. not to return again until 9:30 p.m. was not easy for me. I can't imagine how I would have felt had my body not been ready to walk for twelve hours a day and ride my bike all over a big area. Playing sports helped me to be a better missionary because it prepared my body for the experience.

I was blessed to have a trainer who was incredible. He worked hard, and we had the Spirit. But some days I just longed for a rest. One day, I got my wish and got a rest. My companion had to go with another missionary, so I spent the day with a different missionary. We left the apartment, and he took me shopping for some snacks to put in our pockets to eat while we knocked on doors. While in the store, he bought a big drink, so we sat outside in the car until he finished it. After he downed the drink, he said he needed a quick nap. So we kicked back our seats and tried to sleep. I could not sleep at all. I felt bad inside; I was rested but felt horrible.

Finally we got out and began to knock doors. As we went from house to house, he would stop and ask me about girls at home or my favorite bands. After about two hours of fruitless "work," he told me that he wanted to take me to a place that he thought was the most beautiful place in Pennsylvania. We went to the top of a hill that overlooked a golf course. A mist was hovering over the bright-green, perfectly manicured grass, and deer were grazing on the course. As we sat there, I realized that the whole day had been spent going through the motions, passing time but not using it. I began to feel guilty. Before this evening, all I had wanted was a rest, and now all I wanted was the feeling that I had enjoyed at the end of other days when I was exhausted but satisfied that I had done my best. I realized at that moment that I had left baseball, girls, my mom and her cooking, college, and everything else to do what? Sit with another missionary at a lookout point and watch deer graze on a golf course. That seemed ridiculous to me.

That night I knelt down and repented for not working with "all of my heart, might, mind, and *strength*" that day. What came into my mind as I prayed was this thought: "Heavenly Father, I have always worked so hard at sports. I have always given it my all. This mission is more important to me than my sports career, and I promise that I will work at this the way I worked at sports at home." Whenever I was tempted to stop working, I would think back to all of the times that I felt like stopping in a game, practice, conditioning session, or the weight room and refused to do so. Doing so gave me the courage and resolve to fight through the feeling of wanting to quit while working on my mission. Sports prepared my body for the rigors of missionary work. I did not know how physically demanding a mission would be, but I am grateful that sports prepared me for that rigor.

Growing in Favor with God (Spiritually)

You cannot expect to grow spiritually without doing the work. What work are we talking about? You have to immerse yourself in the scriptures. For some of you, reading the scriptures is a challenge, and understanding them is even harder. You have to work at it. A passive glancing at a few verses a night would be the equivalent of walking around a weight room each morning, flexing in a few mirrors, and expecting your muscles to grow.

A young man we knew shared a story from his mission. He and his companion had a miraculous experience one day. They had finished tracting a street and were on a corner, resting under a tree and waiting for their roommates to pick them up. They felt inspired to return to a street and knock on a few more doors before they were going to be picked up. They wanted to do the work for every minute they could. They knocked on the first door they came to, and a man answered and began to weep. He had just seen a commercial for the Church and went to get a pen to write down the number. He had been baptized eighteen years earlier and had never been back to church. By the time he returned with the pen, the phone number was gone. He got the phonebook and tried to find the Church's number but could not. He even tried to remember the name of the guy that baptized him but could not remember it to look it up in the phonebook. He was frustrated and knelt down and promised God that he would go back to church if he could just find the number. At that moment the two missionaries knocked on his door. The man came back to church, and many of his family members were baptized.

The junior missionary companion stood in the next zone conference and shared this experience. Afterward, the senior companion, who was also a zone leader, was conducting an interview with a missionary from his zone who had been having a hard time working hard. He was a lazy missionary. When asked about how the work was going, he became frustrated. With a red face and clenched teeth, he almost yelled, "If I had experiences like that, I would work hard too." The zone leader responded with a wise answer, "No, Elder, it is the opposite of what you just said. If you worked hard, you would have experiences like that."

That is an important lesson to learn. You don't reap before you sow. In sports, the victory usually comes after the hard work, not before. Likewise, a testimony of the Book of Mormon does not come before you do the work to read, analyze, and apply it; it comes after. A testimony of tithing does not come before you pay it; it comes after you do the work necessary to pay it. Growing spiritually takes work just as it takes work to grow in any other area of your life. The Lord taught that if any man would do his will he would know of the doctrine, whether it be of God or not (see John 7:17). You must do to know. Some want to know before they do, but that is not how it works.

The Bible Dictionary tells us that prayer is a form of work. It reads, "Blessings require some work or effort on our part before we can obtain them. Prayer is a form of work, and is an appointed means for obtaining the highest of all blessings." Once again we realize from this that going through the motions of prayer is not the same thing as sincerely talking with God and trying to discover his will for us. Prayer is more than a passive request; it is a daily battle. In fact, Enos described his experience with prayer as a wrestle. That sounds like more than a "Dear Heavenly Father, I thank thee for this day and for everything. Please bless me in all I do." If you are going to grow spiritually, you will need to do the work when it comes to prayer.

In the Doctrine and Covenants, we are taught that the work of serving in the Church and spreading the gospel of Jesus Christ is a "marvelous work." Why did God call it a marvelous work instead of a marvelous experience? Because it is not just going to happen, most of what is needed to build the kingdom in this last dispensation requires work. Think of our church's terminology for what we do in the kingdom: we do temple *work* and missionary *work*. "Work" is at the heart of this "marvelous *work* and a wonder." We have our Heavenly Father's help and blessings when we seek to "do the marvelous work" necessary to serve and share the gospel truths with others.

Growing in Favor with Man (Socially)

Sports will help you to learn how to work with and bless others. Playing on a team is a wonderful tutoring experience. The lessons learned from getting along with teammates are invaluable. Being part of a team helps you learn to deal with failure without blaming, and to work for success without worrying about who gets the credit. You learn to be unselfish and patient with others and their mistakes. These lessons will help prepare you to deal effectively with your family, friends, mission companions, coworkers, and ward members. It is an invaluable lesson to learn.

Learning to work with others to accomplish a task is so important to being an effective missionary. When there is contention between companions, success is rare. It is vital to learn to work with those who are different than you and to apply the "teamwork" lessons you learned from sports as a missionary.

Another area where the social lessons you learn from sports will bless your life is within the walls of your own home. One misconception that people seem to have nowadays is that relationships, specifically marriage, should be full of sunshine and roses. One bride was reported to have said to her mother when she came out of the temple on her wedding day that she was at the "end of her troubles." Her wise mom backed up, put her hands on her daughter's face, and asked, "Which end?" This mother understood that marriage and family relationships are not easy. Just like becoming a great sports team, becoming a great family takes work.

Another bride-to-be was on her way to the temple to get married. Her dad jokingly said, "Okay, sweetie, if I get off this freeway, the road will go on to eternity. Tell me if you want me to keep going; this is your last chance." She said she sat there and wondered, "Is this going to work?" She went into the temple, knelt across from her fiancé, and was sealed for time and for all eternity. She later said, "At that moment, the question was no longer, 'Is this going to work?' The questions became, 'Heavenly Father, what can I do to make this marriage a wonderful, eternal marriage? How can I make this work?' "

More and more people are quitting when these family relationships get tough. It is important to put effort into our relationships if we want them to be successful. Just as a team has to work together to be successful, a family needs to as well. This is a valuable sports lesson that can be applied to your future social relationships.

Twenty-Second Time-Out

 Do you need to do more work to develop yourself mentally, physically, spiritually, or socially? Ponder which of these four areas you are lacking in the most. What can you specifically do to "do the work" and develop in that area?

_____

_____

_____

_____

_____

_____

_____

_____

_____

_____

Someday Is Not a Day of the Week

We each have Monday through Sunday to do the work, but too many times we put work off to an imaginary day called "Someday." Someday is the day where dreams, goals, and accomplishment go to die. If you are going to be great at sports or anything else, you have to do—not think. You have to act, not plan to act. President Thomas S. Monson has said,

> Professor Harold Hill, in Meredith Willson's *The Music Man*, cautioned, "You pile up enough tomorrows, and you'll find you've collected a lot of empty yesterdays." There is no tomorrow to remember if we don't do something today, and to live most fully today, we must do that which is of greatest importance. Let us not procrastinate those things which matter most. (Thomas S. Monson, "Treasure of Eternal Value," Liahona, Apr. 2008, 2–7.)

A powerful message was given to those who observed the clock hanging above a former NFL coach's desk in his office. Rather than the typical numbers on the clock, the hands had the word "NOW" on them. The message is that there is no need to look up and think, "What time should I . . . ?" The time is now. Just do it now! You will see that the theme of *doing* is laced throughout this book. If we are not doers of the word and are hearers or readers only, our benefit will be limited at best.

In the Book of Mormon, we have a popular scripture about Nephi's response to receiving a pretty hard assignment. He is told to go back into a large city, find a powerful man who doesn't like him, and then somehow get some valuable writings from him. That's not an easy job. What was Nephi's reply to the challenge? "*I will go and do* the things which the Lord has commanded, for I know that the Lord giveth no commandments unto the children of men save he shall prepare a way for them that they may accomplish the thing which he has commanded them" (1 Nephi 3:7, emphasis added).

I WILL GO AND DO! I WILL GO AND DO! No hesitation or "What ifs." I will DO THE WORK because God knows what is best, and he will provide. Will you fail? Well, probably. Nephi failed twice before he obtained the plates.

Will you stop working because you fail? Never! That is what ordinary people do, and you want to be *extraordinary*. You will love and trust your Father! Can you learn to have the same love and then the same passion to want to do and not just know, as Nephi? *YES! You absolutely can, because he loves you and he wants you to succeed.*

The "Do The Work" Challenge

Read over some of the notes you made while pondering the twenty-second time-outs from this chapter. Identify one or two SMART goals that will help you to do the work.

_____

_____

_____

_____

_____

_____

_____

_____

_____

_____

_____

_____

_____

_____

_____

_____

_____
_____
_____
_____
_____
_____
_____
_____
_____
_____
_____
_____
_____
_____
_____
_____
_____
_____
_____
_____
_____

Chapter 2

COMPETE WITHOUT CONTEMPT

Pregame Pep Talk

"I have always loved participating in and attending sporting events. But I confess there are times when the lack of civility in sports is embarrassing. How is it that normally kind and compassionate human beings can be so intolerant and filled with hatred toward an opposing team and its fans? . . . We must realize that all of God's children wear the same jersey. Our team is the brotherhood of man. This mortal life is our playing field. Our goal is to learn to love God and to extend that same love toward our fellowman" (Dieter F. Uchtdorf, "Pride and the Priesthood," *Ensign,* Nov. 2010).

Sports are competitive in nature, and that is not a bad thing—as a matter of fact, the competition is a major factor of why sports are so fun to play. It is hard to be successful in sports unless you have a strong desire to win. Often it is the thrill of winning, or the disappointment of defeat, that drives athletes to do the work. Many wonderful life lessons can be learned from competing in athletics, and we want to be clear that the point of this chapter is not to encourage you to be you to be passive in your desire to be successful or victorious in athletics. There is, however, something to beware of when competing against others: we need to make sure that our competitiveness does not become contempt. To have contempt for something means to have an attitude of utter disgust or hatred for it. As an athlete, you should be able to be a fierce competitor without hating those you compete against. There is nothing wrong with wanting to win. The danger comes when you desire to see another lose or fail.

If you are anything like us, "playing just for fun" is something that is hard to do. Truthfully, sometimes it is annoying to play a sport with someone who is not even trying to compete. There is a level of excitement that comes from trying to win a contest—especially when it is a very competitive contest. The question is, "How can we be great competitors with a drive and a passion for winning without feeling contempt toward those we are competing against?" That is what we would like to talk about in this chapter.

Suggestion #1: Remember the Commandment to Love One Another Applies on the Court and Field

One thing to remember while competing is that those we are competing against are literally our brothers and sisters, and we are commanded to love them. Remembering this will help us to compete without contempt. Sometimes it's easy to forget in the heat of battle. God loves your competitor just as much as he loves you. The more we have played or coached in competitive sports, the more we have come to believe that most often Heavenly Father does not care who wins. He is probably much more interested in how the competitors grow from the experience, represent themselves, and treat each other. The commandments of God still apply on the field or court. Some players and even fans seem to think they can act in a way that is contrary to the commandments when they step on the field. They act as though the fact that they are playing a sport justifies their unrighteous behavior toward their rivals. You cannot take off your "Christian coat" and check it at the door, only to pick it up and put on after the contest is over. We have covenanted to stand as witnesses of God "at all times and in all places," and that includes the field or the court (Mosiah 5:15).

One commandment that is commonly "checked at the door" when it comes to sports is the commandment to love one another. This is not just any commandment either; this commandment is paramount to a Christian life. As a matter of fact, Jesus said that all of the other commandments and all the laws of the prophets hang upon the command to love God and love our neighbor (Matthew 22:40). One of the last sermons Jesus gave in the book of Matthew before he performed the Atonement taught that when you do something (good or bad) unto one of the least of God's children, you have done it unto him (Matthew 25:40–45). Do you think that God's commands are null and void when you compete? Of course not. God did not say "Love one another as I have loved you unless you are competing against them." As hard as it may seem to do, you are commanded to love those you are competing against, even those who for some reason or another are acting like jerks toward you. The Lord has specifically told us to "love our enemies." The definition for enemy in the *Encarta Dictionary* is "unfriendly opponent." That is a great definition in light of this topic. We are to "love our unfriendly opponents," not to mention our friendly ones. You cannot check the commandment to love others at the door.

We recently saw a YouTube video that provided a great example of competing without contempt and loving those you compete against. This event occurred in a college softball game. With two runners on base, a player from Western Oregon University hit what seemed to be a game-winning home run. There was only one problem. In her excitement, she missed first base. As she turned back to touch the base, she crumbled to the ground with a serious knee injury. The injury was bad enough that she could not continue around the bases. Under the rules, her own team was prohibited from assisting her and she lay on the ground crying and holding her knee.

That is when it occurred. Two players from the opposite team did something that showed they understood the importance of competing without contempt. Though they were devastated at losing the game, which also ended their hopes of competing in the playoffs, the first baseman and the shortstop picked up their opponent and traveled from base to base, lowering their opponent to touch each of them.

One of them said of the moment, "In the end, it is not about winning and losing so much. It was about this girl. She hit it over the fence and was in pain, and she deserved a home run" (http://nbcsports.msnbc.com/id/24392612/).

What a great example of competing without contempt.

Twenty-Second Time-Out

Ponder this: Have you ever "checked your religion" at the door of an athletic contest? How did you treat people in your last game, such as your opponents, referees, teammates who messed up, and so on?

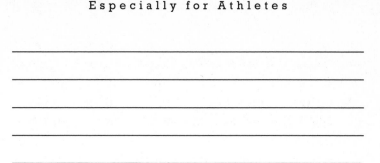

Suggestion #2: Appreciate the Greatness of Your Opponent While Trying to Win

Another way we can avoid feeling contempt toward those we are competing against is to learn to admire and appreciate their skill and greatness. How do we do that? There is a scripture story that we think sheds some light on the answer to this question. The chief governor of the Nephites during the time of captain Moroni was a man named Pahoran. Pahoran ended up being a righteous man, but Moroni was frustrated at the lack of support his armies were getting from Pahoran and the government. He wrote a condemning letter to Pahoran. In it he said that thousands had died because of Pahoran's great neglect and wickedness. He accused him of sitting upon his throne in the heart of the land surrounded by security and letting the soldiers die to protect his freedom without even giving them food to sustain them. He concluded his letter by saying in so many words, "send us help or I will come kill you myself."

What Captain Moroni did not know was that Pahoran was having a battle of his own, and that the reason he was not helping was because some of Pahoran's own people had risen up against him and tried to overthrow the government. He was busy fighting that battle in the land of Zarahemla and that is why he could not send assistance to Moroni's men.

You might be wondering at this point what in the world

this has to do with competing in athletics. The part of this story that is impressive and applicable is Pahoran's response to Moroni. After explaining the situation in Zarahemla and why he had not been able to send assistance to Moroni and his soldiers, Pahoran said, "And now, in your epistle you have censured me, but it mattereth not; I am not angry, but do rejoice in the greatness of your heart" (Alma 61:9). What an awesome attitude. In the midst of this conflict, Pahoran could have said, "Shut it, Moroni. You have no idea what we are going through. Say something like that again, and I will come after you." Instead, he looked at Moroni and saw something in him that he admired. He appreciated the greatness of his heart. He was glad he had a man like that leading his army.

There are a lot of differences between Moroni and Pahoran's exchange on the battlefields and the exchanges that you will participate in on the field of play; however, the ability to "rejoice in the greatness" of your opponent is something that will help you compete without contempt.

The ability to admire and respect an opponent while trying with all of your heart to win is an important ability for a Christian athlete to posses. With this attitude you will have good sportsmanship. You will be able to compliment your opponents on a nice shot or tackle or hit. Of course you will want to beat them, but you will not want to hurt or demean them. When you knock them down, you will extend a hand to pick them up instead of stand over them in an attempt to show them up. You will want to leave everything out on the field, but, win or lose, you will shake their hands after the game without any ill feelings toward them. You may hate to lose, but that is a lot different than hating those who beat you. With this attitude, you will feel bad for individuals who may have been hurt or missed the play that lost the game for their team because you love them and know how it feels to be in that situation.

Here are a couple of stories from Dustin's life that help to demonstrate what the "compete without contempt" principle looks like in action.

Dustin's Story

Years before competing in high school and college, and before coaching high school and college athletes, I learned a valuable lesson on how to compete without contempt. I learned this lesson on the baseball field when I was only thirteen years old. I hope that by sharing this, others may learn a similar lesson as the lesson I learned that hot summer afternoon.

One of the greatest joys a young baseball player can have is the joy of being picked to play on the all-star team after the regular season finishes. When I was thirteen, the all-star experience was something that those of us chosen knew had the opportunity to be a special one. We had a great team, and through the first couple rounds of the state tournament representing the Sandy East Pony League, we were winning by ten or more runs each game. In the final game to decide who would represent Utah in the Western Regional tournament, we again took control of the game early and had a lead of several runs late into the game. I was pitching a shutout, had already hit a home run, and couldn't wait to talk with my dad after the game! Late in the game, I was on second base, and my teammate hit a ball into the outfield. I ran to third base and was told to round the base and head for home. When I approached home, the catcher had positioned himself in front of the plate to block my being able to slide and reach the plate. My only option was to lower my shoulder and plow into the catcher, hoping that by doing so he would not be able to hold on to the incoming ball and tag me out, and I would be able to touch the plate and earn the run for my team. I had seen this done before by the pros on TV and we had even practiced it at practice. It was a legal play, and I was determined to not allow him to stop me from reaching home plate. I was at full speed with my left shoulder and forearm tucked, and I hit into him right below his chin. I was safe! He was on his back with his catcher's mask crooked across his face and the ball rolling several feet away from him. What I did in that moment was very telling of my attitude at the time. Rather than helping him up, I showed him up. With my teammates cheering and running out of the dugout to meet me with high fives and hugs, I, with the catcher underneath me, stood up, looked directly down at him, and—while pointing at him with both hands—yelled as loud as I could. Rather than being compassionate, I was arrogant; rather than respecting my opponent, I chose to draw attention to myself.

We won the game, I was given a large trophy, and we were all set as a team to head out of state to represent Utah. I met my dad behind the field and as a good dad should do, he hugged me, congratulated me for playing well, and then said with disappointment in his eyes, "What a game son, but did you have to stand over and point at the catcher like that?" He was right, and I was embarrassed. I did the wrong thing, and to this day I regret it. I regret treating a fellow competitor that way. I regret not being a better example to my teammates. I regret disrespecting my parents, my coaches, and my community. I am sure Father in Heaven expected more out of me. I did the work, but my eyes were not up.

I made a deal with my dad that I would show better respect for my opponent, and even went as far as to agree to my dad's invitation to shake the hand of any player to hit a home run off of me as he rounded third base on his way for home. Unfortunately for my team, I had the opportunity to do that twice over the next several years. I would, however, much rather feel the humility of shaking the hand of a player who just hit a home run off of me than see the disappointment in the eyes of those who I looked up to like my coaches, my dad, or my Father in Heaven for doing something as selfish as what I did that summer day on the baseball field.

In the fall of 1995, two very good high school football players went from rivals to friends in front of thousands of people one night and showed how athletes can compete without contempt. One was a hard-hitting, super-competitive strong safety from the state's top football program in the heart of a big city. The other was a nimble, lightning-fast wide receiver from a brand-new high school in a small town. The two first met early in the season in a very competitive game. The wide receiver and his new team got the win against the proud and confident team from the big city, shocking a lot of people.

For the next ten weeks, it became more and more apparent that their paths would cross again in the playoffs since both teams reeled off impressive winning streaks. At the end of the regular season, both teams entered the playoffs as number-one seeds. Sure enough, both teams rolled through the playoffs and met in the state championship game, which was televised throughout the state on a major TV station. The game was close throughout and in overtime came down to one final play. Facing a fourth down and ten yards to go, the small town team needed a touchdown to win. The play was designed for the gifted wide receiver to work across the back of the end zone while other routes ran underneath him, causing confusion and allowing him to get open in the back corner. The play worked perfectly. The pass was perfectly thrown, and the strong safety was not there in time to knock it away. The ball hit the sure-handed receiver squarely in the hands for what should have been the game-winning catch and the state championship victory. The receiver bobbled it twice and, to everyone's surprise, dropped the ball. The game was over.

Imagine the range of emotions that each player must have felt in the fraction of a second it took for the ball to fall from the receiver's hands to the ground. The strong safety changed

in emotion from what looked like defeat and disappointment to sudden joy and elation, and the wide receiver from
assured triumph and applause to disappointment and defeat.
How would you have acted if you were the strong safety? How
did Heavenly Father feel at this moment? Father in Heaven
must have been in a difficult position. Of course, he would
be thrilled seeing the joy of one of his sons as he celebrated a
lifetime achievement and the title of state champion, but what
about his other son? He was just as deserving, yet he fell to
his knees and dropped his head into his hands, completely
humiliated in front of thousands of people both at the stadium
and watching on TV. I believe it is safe to assume that our
Heavenly Father hoped the winning competitor would choose
to handle the chaotic moment with class and to show love to
his opponent, who, although wearing another color jersey, was
his brother. Some may have pounded their chests or rubbed
it in to their competitors. Others would have ran and joined
their team and celebrated their wonderful accomplishment.

What did this young man do? He chose not to run to
teammates and celebrate; rather, he joined his opponent on
one knee, put his arm around his shoulder, and spoke a word
of comfort to the defeated young man, telling him he had
nothing to be ashamed of and that he was the reason his team
had done as well as they had that year. He remained at his side
for several seconds and postponed celebrating what must have
been one of the greatest feelings of his sports career in order
show love and concern for his opponent. When the TV picked
up the scene and remained focused on this sign of sportsmanship, it lead to dozens of letters of praise and appreciation from
viewers to the coaches and schools of both young men, thank-
ing them for showing the kind of class they hoped all athletes would express in such a moment. Later the two young
men met for a photo shoot, and the story was told in a LDS
church magazine. To this day, this story is shared in Sunday

School lessons and seminary classes. The two young men both postponed opportunities to continue their sports career and schooling after high school to serve missions and share with others the wonderful gospel of Jesus Christ. They taught thousands of people on that cold November night that it is possible to compete without contempt, to win while giving aid to the humiliated, embarrassed, and defeated. I am confident Heavenly Father smiled on that moment and that both young men were blessed by the experience.

The young man who chose to take the knee and give support was my brother, and I watched the event on TV in a dorm room in college. Few times in my life have I ever been as proud.

We want to be clear about something here. Competing without contempt is not just something that happens in state championship games when everyone is watching. Some of you reading this book will have the opportunity to play on big stages but all of us will compete in city parks, front yards, and driveways. Is this principle any less relevant in those places? Some of our most competitive moments in our sports career happened on Cedar Crest Drive, 17th Street East and Rose Marie Ave. They were not against our rivals; in fact, they were against our closest friends and family members. For Shad, it was battles against Chris, Sheldon, Shawn, Shane, and Adam. For Dustin, it was Nate and Ryan, Shelby, Landon, Dave, Jeff, and the late Scott Warner, who passed away on his way home from a football game his senior year. Why do we mention these names here? These are still some of our best friends in the world. It is tragic enough to compete with contempt against a rival, but when you compete with contempt against your best friends you put friendships at risk. When you want to win so bad that you start feeling contempt toward your friends, remember you will never regret erring on the side of friendship.

Twenty-Second Time-Out

Think of one of your competitors that you really admire. How can you maintain that respect for them and "appreciate their greatness" while still competing against them?

_____

_____

_____

_____

_____

_____

_____

_____

_____

Off-the-Field Applications

If you can learn now to compete in a righteous way, it will serve you well your whole life. President Gordon B. Hinckley said to the youth of the Church, "You are moving into the most competitive age the world has ever known. All around you is competition" (Gordon B. Hinckley, "A Prophet's Counsel and Prayer for Youth," _New Era_, Jan. 2001, 4). He then talked about the importance of gaining an education and marketable skills.

School is an area where you need to learn to compete without contempt. As you strive to get good grades, get accepted to colleges, and receive scholarships, you may be tempted to have negative feelings toward those you are competing against. Some teachers even grade on a curve, pitting students against each other. You can react to those feelings in many different ways. Some make those they are competing against their rivals or their enemies. Some choose to put others down; others choose to cheat in order to get a leg up. What is best? It is best to learn to love those you are competing against and do all that you can to be your best.

As you go forward in life, you will have to compete for jobs, for customers, maybe for the heart of the one you love, and for many other good things. Learning to compete without contempt while playing sports in your youth will be a blessing to you as you move into the competitive world President Hinckley was talking about. If you remember that all of the commandments still apply, that we are all brothers and sisters, and that you can appreciate the greatness and recognize the good in your competitors, you will be able to compete without contempt throughout your life.

In review, you should want to perform at your highest level. Striving to be your best is definitely encouraged; however, doing so with a hope that the opposition is left destroyed and embarrassed is not Christlike. Win or lose, you should never check your religion at the door; all of the commandments still apply. You should win or lose with dignity and honor. You should always strive to be an example of him who won the greatest victory of all. He conquered death and hell on our behalf because of the love he had for us. You should love others the way he loved you, even when competing against them.

The "Do the Work" Challenge

Read over some of the notes you made while pondering the twenty-second time-outs from this chapter. Identify one or two SMART goals that will help you to compete without contempt.

_____

_____

_____

_____

_____

_____

_____

_____

_____

_____

_____

_____

_____

_____

_____

_____

_____

_____

_____

_____

Especially for Athletes

_____
_____
_____
_____
_____
_____
_____
_____
_____
_____
_____
_____
_____
_____
_____
_____
_____
_____
_____
_____
_____
_____
_____
_____
_____
_____

Chapter 3:

SEEK TO BLESS, NOT TO IMPRESS

Pregame Pep Talk

> "Most anyone can stand adversity, but to test
> a man's character give him power."
> **—Abraham Lincoln**

> "Leadership is power. How you handle that power—or how
> power handles you—reveals your character."
> **—John Wooden**

> "Talent is God given—be humble
> Fame is man-given—be thankful
> Conceit is self-given—be careful."
> **—Source unknown**

The Lord will magnify the talents of those who choose to use their talents to bless others. When speaking of spiritual gifts in the forty-sixth section of the Doctrine and Covenants, the Lord said that he gives individuals spiritual gifts so that "all may be profited thereby." In other words, he gave you your gifts to bless others—not just to impress others. When we were teenage athletes, we did not view our athleticism as a spiritual gift. But we believe athleticism is a gift from

God. Like any other gift, God expects us to use that gift to bless others, this chapter will discuss how we can do so.

The "Sportlight"

We would like to reintroduce a phrase here, something we like to call the "sportlight." "Sportlight" refers to the time in your life when the spotlight seems to be on you a little bit more than normal because you play sports. It is the time when people see you and notice what you do on and off the field. It is the time when little kids watch you play, dreaming of someday being in your shoes and doing what you do. Some seem to like the sportlight, but a special few do more than enjoy the attention; they recognize at a young age that they can take this "sportlight" and use it to bless and lift others instead of just impress them. You can either use the sportlight to persuade others do good, or you can use it otherwise. The Lord will magnify your talents if you use the sportlight to do good. What will others see when the sportlight shines upon you?

Twenty-Second Time-Out

When the "sportlight" shines on you, what do others see? Can you think of a time when you tried to impress others instead of bless others? What could you have done differently?

_____

_____

_____

_____

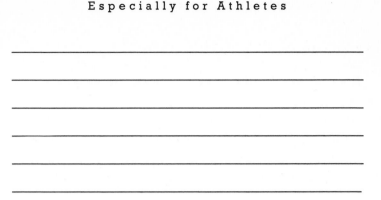

You Can't Choose to Turn Off the Sportlight

One thing you can't do is decide that you don't want the sportlight—that you don't want to be a role model. You have no choice. People will look up to and admire you, and little kids will try to be like you. One choice you do have is whether you will seek to bless or impress during your time in the sportlight. You may be familiar with the parable of the talents. Talents were money in the Savior's day. In this parable, a man is leaving on a long journey, and he distributes his talents to three men to watch over while he is gone. To the first man, he gave five talents; to the second, two; and to the third man, he gave one. When he came back, the first man gave him the good news that he had taken the five talents and had gained five more talents. The second man had taken the two talents and delivered back to the man two additional talents. The lord was pleased with them and promised to make them rulers over even more.

Sadly, the third man, who was given one talent, informed the Lord that he was afraid so he took his talent and hid it in the earth. The lord's response teaches us a great lesson, "Thou wicked and slothful servant. . . . Take therefore the talent from him, and give it unto him which hath ten talents" (Matthew

25:14–28). Talents are referring to money here, but I think the principle can apply to the way we use the word "talents" today. The Lord expects us to take the talents that he gives us and do good with them. Notice that the man who was rebuked in the parable did not do anything bad with his talent; he simply did nothing at all. Of course, some will use their time in the spotlight to do bad things. They may use their popularity or strength to bully others or to persuade them to do bad things. This would obviously be disappointing to the Lord. We should recognize, however, that doing nothing, or not as much as we could have with our talent, is also disappointing to the Lord. On the other hand, notice what the Lord does with those who take the talents he gives them and uses them to do good things. He gives them even more talents. If we do use our talents to do good things, the Lord will magnify and multiply our talents. In other words, if you use the spotlight that is upon you to bless others, God will multiply your talents.

So what are some of the good things you can do with the spotlight? Here are a couple of examples.

As a freshman in high school, Chris made the varsity baseball team where he made an impact on the team from the moment he stepped on the field. His swing was so sweet, you would see people in the stands turn and look at each other in amazement when he hit the ball. When he went to a baseball camp at Pepperdine University as a sophomore in high school, he stepped into the batter's box, and one of the college players threw him a pitch. He drove the ball deep into the outfield. The guy who threw the pitch and one of the Pepperdine coaches simultaneously said, "Hello, Chris." Chris led his team to two championships, was an all-league performer all four years of his high school career, set numerous school and state records, and received a full-ride baseball scholarship to Cal State Northridge, which he turned down when he was drafted by the Baltimore Orioles.

As impressive as Chris was on the field, he was more impressive off the field. There was a special needs girl named Julie at his school. Throughout junior high, she would often pick a young man to have a crush on and then follow that person around, doing some pretty socially awkward things to get his attention. When Chris was a freshman, she chose to follow him, but this time her crush stuck for almost four years, probably because Chris was such a good person that he never made fun of her or belittled her. As his high school days were closing, Chris went to prom with a nice girl and a group of friends. At some point during the prom, Chris noticed that Julie was there. She had chosen to come to prom without a date, and she was hovering around the dance floor, watching Chris's every move.

Suddenly Chris was gone. His friends could not find him anywhere. A few of his friends went to take pictures. As they walked into the room where the photographer was, there was Chris standing next to Julie, holding her hand and posing for a picture. I wish you could have seen Julie's face. She was beaming. He then took her to the dance floor and danced with her and then politely excused himself and returned to his date. When people complimented him, he brushed it off as though it was nothing and just the right thing to do. He never talked about it again.

Chris is a great example of someone who used the sport-light to bless others and not to impress others. As his friends witnessed what he did, it gave them the desire to treat others they way he treated Julie that night. It had an especially big impact on the young players from his team who witnessed this event. Some people who are as talented as Chris think that their talent gives them license to put others down or to point out as often as possible how much "better" or more important they are than those around them. Others, like Chris, realize that their position as athletes gives them the opportunity to lift, help, and protect others.

ESPN wrote an article about another young man who understood this principle of blessing others. His name is Carson Jones. Carson is the quarterback of a state championship football team in Arizona. There is a young lady with special needs named Chy at his school. The article quoted Chy's mother, who said, "She'd come home every night at the start of the school year crying and upset. That permanent smile she had, that gleam in her eye, that was all gone." Chy's mother wrote Carson a Facebook message asking him to keep an eye on her. He did a lot more than that. He befriended her. He invited her to sit with him and his friends at lunch, and she started to help out with the football team. In short, this young man changed this girl's life. She went from crying every night to writing "Lucky Girl" on a card she made for Carson (http://espn.go.com/espn/story/_/id/8579599/chy-johnson-boys).

Ordinary people think it is a noble thing just to not pick on those who are less fortunate than they are. That is definitely better than picking on someone, but remember the parable of the talents. The man with one talent was chastised for doing nothing with his talent. Extraordinary people, like Carson and Chris, realize that they can do more than merely refrain from putting others down; they use their talents and position in life to lift others up. We must confess that this is a lesson we wish we would have understood better. We were never ones to pick on others, but at times we were a little too ordinary. Don't be as we were. Don't be ordinary. Use your time in the sportlight to lift others, to protect others, and to bless others, not just to impress others.

Twenty-Second Time-Out

Think about one person at school, in your ward, on your team, or in your family that you could bless because of your position in the sportlight. Write down his or her name and something that you can do for him or her.

_____

_____

_____

_____

_____

_____

_____

_____

_____

_____

Seeking to Bless Instead of Impress Makes You a Better Teammate

Maybe all of us have had the unfortunate opportunity to play with those who thought the game was all about them. They did as much as they possibly could to draw attention to themselves, and they viewed others—even teammates—who received attention as their enemies. People who struggle with this have a hard time being a good teammate. They live with the sorry attitude, "If you succeed, I am a failure" (Ezra Taft Benson, "Beware of Pride," *Ensign*, May 1989). This attitude manifests itself in many ways on the field of play. It is the root of "ball hogging" and "chest thumping" and attracting attention to every good thing one does on the field. It is often the root of dissension in the locker room or complaining behind the coaches back.

The problem of wanting attention and praise to the point that it is damaging to those around us is not a new problem; it is as old as the Old Testament. Saul was a man that was revered and honored in Israel and had done many good things there. He was a fine man when he was on top and when all of the people were looking up to him. Then came a giant man of the Philistines named Goliath. Day after day he challenged the Israelites to send a man down to do battle with him but no one, including Saul who the scriptures tell us was a very large man, would take the challenge. Eventually, David, a young shepherd boy, went down with a sling and some smooth stones to take on Goliath. Exhibiting great faith and bravery, David defeated Goliath, causing the Philistines to become afraid and retreat. Instantly David became famous in Israel. You would think that King Saul would have loved David for being so brave in defense of his people. But when the Israelite women began to dance and sing, "Saul hath slain his thousands, and David his ten thousands," Saul became angry, and the scriptures tell us that "Saul eyed David from that day and forward" (1 Samuel 18:7–9). On many occasions Saul even tried to kill David. What happened to make Saul act this way? He was so bugged because the women seemed to be more impressed with David than they were with him. Saul obviously was more concerned with impressing others than he was with blessing others.

Those Saul-like attitudes manifest themselves in sports as well. When we worry about who gets the credit for the victory or the tackle or the goal, or who is written about in the paper, or who makes the all-region team, we are worrying more about impressing than we are about blessing. As in all things, our perfect example of how we should be is the Savior Jesus. He never did what he did to impress others. In fact, many times after healing someone he would say something to the effect of "see that no man knows it." He was not worried about getting the credit for the things he did and went out of his way to deflect credit and praise. One of these occasions when he deflected praise was when he raised Lazarus from the dead. He must have known that the people around would be amazed when they saw a man who had been dead for four days walk out of a tomb. What did he do? Before he went down into the tomb, he paused outside, looked up toward heaven, and said, "Father, I thank thee that thou hast heard me" (John 11:41). Why did the Savior say that before he went down into the tomb and raised a man who had been there for four days from the dead? We believe it was because Jesus wanted the people to give credit to his Father.

What a blessing you could be to a team if you were always hoping for and helping those around you to do their best. When you have a Saul-like attitude, it undermines, divides, and weakens your team. On the other hand, when you are a team-first person, one who helps those around you to succeed, you make everyone around you better and are pleased to see them succeed. You are not worried about who gets the credit or the ball, you are worried about the team. You are worried about blessing not impressing.

Twenty-Second Time-Out

What is something that you have done in the past to try to attract undue attention to yourself that you can stop doing? How will seeking to bless others rather than impress others make you a better teammate?

_____

_____

_____

_____

_____

_____

_____

_____

_____

_____

_____

Seeking to Bless Instead of Impress Helps Us Use Our Gifts as We Were Intended To

One of the scripture stories that teaches this principle is the story of Samson in the Old Testament. Prior to Samson's birth, the Israelites had been ruled by the Philistines for forty years. An angel appeared to Samson's mother, who had not been able to have children, and told her that she would have a son that would "begin to deliver Israel out of the hand of the Philistines" (Judges 13:5).

Samson was born with an extreme amount of strength. Early in his life he killed a young lion with his bare hands. However, it seems that one of Samson's problems was that he forgot why he was blessed with such great strength. He seemed to forget that his strength was given him to "begin to deliver Israel," in other words, to bless others. Instead it seemed that he almost always used his strength for his own purposes. He killed thirty Philistines and took their clothing and bedding to pay off a debt he incurred when they figured out a riddle and, in essence, won a bet. When his father-in-law gave his wife to another man he decided to catch some foxes, light their tails on fire, and set them loose in the corn fields of the Philistines, burning them down. When the Philistines found out he had done so out of anger toward his father-in-law and wife, the Philistines had them killed. This enraged Samson more, and he smote them with a great slaughter (Judges 14–15). He died in one last fit of anger when he pulled down some pillars, collapsing a building upon himself and those who had gathered to mock him. We have been unable to find an instance in Samson's life where he used his great strength to help someone else.

Do you use the talent you have been blessed with to play sports to lift and help others or to lift and help yourself? It is okay to want to excel; the problem sometimes lies in *why* we want to excel. Forget about making yourself look good, and try to make others feel good.

Receiving Attention Is Not a Sign That You Are Not Living This Principle

This principle of seeking to bless, not impress, like most others, can be taken too far. The message is not to dumb yourself down or not seek to be an impressive individual. The concern is with why we want to impress, not that we want to be impressive. We want to be impressive individuals and athletes for the intent to do good. The Savior taught a similar principle regarding riches. He said, "But before ye seek for riches seek ye for the kingdom of God . . . and ye will seek them for the intent to do good—to clothe the naked, and to feed the hungry, and to liberate the captive, and to administer relief to the sick and the afflicted" (Jacob 2:18–19). It is not bad to want to be financially successful as long as it is for the right reasons. I think we can change a few words in that scripture and apply it to sports. We might say, "But before ye seek to excel at sports seek ye for the kingdom of God . . . and ye will seek to excel at sports for the intent to do good."

The irony may be that when someone seeks to bless others instead of impress them they become more impressive. In Matthew chapters 5–7 Jesus taught the people the Sermon on the Mount. Many of the things he taught surrounded the principle that we should not do what we do to be seen of men and attract attention to ourselves, rather we should do what we do to glorify God. At the conclusion of his teaching, Jesus left the mountain. And the next verse records that, "great multitudes followed him" (Matthew 8:1). Obviously the people were impressed with the Savior. Had he done something wrong? Of course not. People who seek to bless instead of impress have a magnetic personality that attracts others to them because they began to sense that when they are around such a person they themselves become better.

This principle is something that is deep within you and something that drives the way you think, act, and feel. It is not as shallow as simply pointing to heaven when you do something good in a game, or "Tebowing" after a touchdown. It is not pretending to be humble when you know you have had a great game and someone gives you a compliment. It is so much more than that. It is anxiously and prayerfully seeking to use your God-given abilities to bless others.

Off-the-Field Applications

It is pretty easy to see how this principle applies to more than just sports. If you can learn to think and act in order to bless others instead of impress them, you will be more prosperous in every area of your life. Let's talk about a few specific areas though.

Missionaries that have learned this principle will do what they do in order to bless those they have been called to serve, instead of to impress the mission president, parents, or the girl or boy at home. When we seek to impress others as a missionary, we are at the mercy of their standards. If it is impressive to be spiritual we will be spiritual, if it is impressive to act a little rebellious, we will do that too. If we have a companion that likes to work, we will work; if we have a disobedient companion, we will be disobedient. If we are teaching someone that loves the church, we will too; when someone is being critical of the church we may feel tempted to dumb down our testimony or not bear it at all. We become like a chameleon, changing colors to blend in wherever we are.

When you seek to bless others as a missionary, you become a rock. You are not swayed by what others will think because you are interested in blessing them not impressing them. You will act the same way no matter who you are around. You will not be afraid of others dropping in on your apartment or asking you about your day. You will act the same way around the mission president as you would when no one is around.

Employees that have learned this lesson will strive to build the company and serve those they are paid to serve rather than trying undermine those they are in competition with. They will not worry about *appearing* to work hard; they *will* work hard. They will not be interested in formulating excuses when things go wrong, they will use their energy to formulate solutions because they are more concerned with the company succeeding than they are about who gets blamed for failures or mistakes. You can see how this applies to so many of life's situations.

The Savior Jesus Christ is the greatest of all. He had all power and ability. If anyone ever had the right to feel and act like they were better than others, it would have been him. But he did not use his power and abilities to impress others or to outdo others. He constantly tried to bless others. No one was beneath him. He was often accused of eating with publicans and sinners and spending time with the lame and blind and leprous. He knew who he was and was only ever interested in impressing and pleasing one person: His Father. Consequently he was the greatest being who ever walked the face of this earth. As an athlete you have been given a gift. At this time when you are in the sportlight, we hope that you will learn to use that opportunity to do good and lift those around you and to inspire in a positive way those who will look up to you. We hope that the sportlight never makes you feel better than anyone. You are not. Living the way the Savior lived his life will help you to live without regret. If you will seek to bless instead of impress, God will help you to become all that he intends you to become, and, like the men who did well with the talents they were given, you will hear, "well done thou good and faithful servant."

The "Do The Work" Challenge

Read over some of the notes you made while pondering the twenty-second time-outs from this chapter. Identify one or two SMART goals that will help you to seek to bless instead of impress others.

_____

_____

_____

_____
_____
_____
_____
_____
_____
_____
_____
_____
_____
_____
_____
_____
_____
_____
_____
_____
_____
_____
_____
_____
_____
_____
_____
_____

_____

_____

_____

_____

_____

_____

Chapter 4

FIRST THINGS FIRST

Pregame Pep Talk

> "Action expresses priorities."
> **—Mahatma Gandhi**

> "Things which matter most must never be at the mercy of things which matter least."
> **—Johann Wolfgang von Goethe**

> "Desires dictate our priorities, priorities shape our choices, and choices determine our actions."
> **—Dallin H. Oaks**

> "When we put God first, all other things fall into their proper place or drop out of our lives. Our love of the Lord will govern the claims for our affection, the demands on our time, the interests we pursue, and the order of our priorities."
> **—Ezra Taft Benson**

If you are anything like us, you could eat, drink, and sleep sports. We remember sitting in class as elementary kids and drawing baseball fields or football plays in our notebooks and eagerly anticipating recess when we could go out and play sports. We also remember the disappointment we would feel when the bell would ring and it was time to go back to class. Sometimes, it seemed like torture to stay inside on Sunday instead of going outside and playing sports. This highlights one of the dangers of loving sports so much. You may be tempted to make sports too big of a part of your life. Sports are great, and many lessons can be learned from them, but if they become too important, they may begin to push some of the more important things out of your life.

BYU football coach Bronco Mendenhall has received some criticism the last couple of years because he has stated that football should be fifth on his team's priority list. He says that faith, family, knowledge, and friends should come before football. Some have blasted coach Mendenhall for this philosophy and mocked him over and over again for it. Our question is, which of those should football come before? Faith? Your family? Knowledge (schooling)? Friends? It does not feel right to most rational people to put football or any other sport above any of those things.

Elder Richard G. Scott asked some questions regarding the topic of putting first things first. We think they are great for those who love sports as much as we do to consider. He asked,

> Are there so many fascinating, exciting things to do or so many challenges pressing down upon you that it is hard to keep focused on that which is essential? When things of the world crowd in, all too often the wrong things take highest priority. Then it is easy to forget the fundamental purpose of life. Satan has a powerful tool to use against good people. It is distraction. He would have good people fill life with 'good things' so there is no room for the essential ones. Have you unconsciously been caught in that trap? (Richard G. Scott, "First Things First," *Ensign*, May 2001, 6)

What a wonderful soul-searching quote. Let's adjust the quote to talk specifically about sports. Are there so many fascinating, exciting sports to play or so many challenges pressing down upon you that it is hard to keep focused on that which is essential? When you become too focused on sports, all too often the wrong things take highest priority. Then it is easy to forget the fundamental purpose of life. Satan has a powerful tool to use against good athletes. It is distraction. He would have athletes fill life with so many sports so there is no room for the essential things. Have you unconsciously been caught in that trap?

In that same vein, Elder Dallin H. Oaks gave a talk entitled "Good, Better, Best." He said that some things in life are good, others are better, but some are best, and we should make sure that we are making time for the best things in our lives. In that talk he said, "We should begin by recognizing the reality that just because something is *good* is not a sufficient reason for doing it. The number of good things we can do far exceeds the time available to accomplish them. Some things are better than good, and these are the things that should command priority attention in our lives" (Dallin H. Oaks, "Good, Better, Best," *Ensign*, Nov. 2007, 104–8).

Examples of Ways That Sports Can Become Too Important in Our Lives

Sometimes the greatest enemy to great is good. Sports are good. The whole premise of this book is based upon the fact that sports can provide wonderful growing opportunities to the athletes. This book talks some about becoming better at sports, but the main point of this book is that sports can help you become better in more important areas of your life. There are many people in the world who are great when it comes to sports but they don't have a very good life otherwise. The hard part in all of this is that it is ordinary to give priority to things that entertain you. But remember the goal is not to be ordinary. The goal is to be extraordinary, and extraordinary people put first things first. We don't want you to have a good life. We want you to have a great life. Learning to put first things first in your life is an important part of having a great life. What does it look like when sports become too important? Let's look at a few choices you may need to make in your sports career where this principle of putting first things first will need to be applied.

Sports and the Sabbath

As the world moves ever and ever further from viewing Sunday as a holy day and moves toward viewing it as a holiday, you will inevitably be faced with the choice of whether or not you will play on Sundays. What is more important? What should take the highest priority here: Taking time to pause and remember the atoning sacrifice of Jesus Christ and renew our covenants with him, or to play in a game?

Elder Neil L. Anderson told the story in general conference of an incredible rugby player named Sid Going. Sid was invited to play on the most celebrated rugby team in the world, the All Blacks of New Zealand. He chose to forgo this opportunity to serve a mission but was able to resume his career and become very successful after his mission. Elder Anderson said a line that struck us in his talk. He said, "How good was Sid Going? He was so good that training and game schedules were changed because he would not play on Sunday" (Neil L. Anderson, "Preparing the World for the Second Coming," *Ensign*, May 2011). Can you imagine what would happen if more athletes refused to play on Sundays? Even at a young age if you were to put first things first and observe the Sabbath, more coaches would strive to get games to be scheduled on other days of the week. Decide now that you will put first things first by never putting sports ahead of the Sabbath. Doing so will make it easier to make the decision when the time of decision comes. It is harder to make a decision in the moment.

Sports Ahead of Missions and Church Service

One of the decisions that face many LDS athletes is whether or not to forgo their sports career for two years and serve a mission. President Monson said recently, "I repeat what prophets have long taught—that every worthy, able young man should prepare to serve a mission. Missionary service is a priesthood duty—an obligation the Lord expects of us who have been given so very much" (Thomas S. Monson, "As We Meet Together Again," *Ensign*, Nov. 2010). We think it is important to emphasize the word every. The Lord needs servants who are worthy and able to serve him. As we have mentioned previously, playing sports has blessed your life and prepared you to serve the Lord in the mission field. The Lord said during his ministry that, "The harvest truly is plenteous, but the labourers are few; Pray ye therefore the Lord of the harvest, that he will send forth labourers into his harvest" (Matthew 9:37–38). What an honor to be one of the few who are willing to serve the Lord.

Some will tell you that you can do more missionary work by staying home and being a stand-out athlete. That line of thinking has a flaw to it though. It seems to assume that you cannot do both. President Benson has taught that "Men and women who turn their lives over to God will discover that He can make a lot more out of their lives than they can. He will deepen their joys, expand their vision, quicken their minds, strengthen their muscles, lift their spirits, multiply their blessings, increase their opportunities, comfort their souls, raise up friends, and pour out peace." (Ezra Taft Benson, *Teachings of Ezra Taft Benson*, Salt Lake City: Bookcraft, 1988, 361) You will never go wrong by turning your life over to God for those two years of a mission. Doing so will help you become all that you were supposed to become. If that includes athletics, the Lord will bless you with the opportunities to play athletics.

He is on your side and will give you what is best for you if you have the faith to turn your life over to him.

Shad's Experience

I realized during my sophomore year of high school that I might have an opportunity to play baseball beyond high school. I was being invited to play on some scout teams, and I had talked with a few scouts and received letters from a few colleges. I was very excited, and this became so important to me that the most important things took a backseat. I loved the Church, the prophet, Joseph Smith, the Book of Mormon, and most important, Jesus Christ; however, I fear that during this portion of my life, I had let the wrong things take the highest priority. I was not putting first things first.

I have always had a sensitive conscience. I feel really bad when I am involved in something wrong. I remember days when I was out playing ball on a Sunday when I would have a nagging pain in my heart because I knew I was not where I was supposed to be. For this and other reasons, I knelt down one evening late in the night to pray and ask Heavenly Father if I was okay and to find out what my standing was in his eyes. I had one of the strongest spiritual impressions that I have ever received that I should prepare to serve a mission. I had just signed my letter of intent to play baseball at Cal State Los Angeles. After talking with my father, I decided to honor the commitment I had made to Cal State LA for my freshman year and then prepare to serve a mission.

I enrolled in and began attending Cal State LA in the fall of 1995. The adversary instantly began to work on me through peer pressure, girls, and pride. I was constantly surrounded by temptations. It was really hard to hold on to those spiritual experiences I had undergone, and sometimes it was really hard to feel the Spirit in that environment.

I went home for Christmas—we had almost a month

break—and it felt so good to be home and not surrounded by so many temptations. I made some resolutions that I thought would help me live in the world and not be affected by it so much. I made commitments to read my scriptures and pray.

The season began, and I was not in the starting lineup our first game. At first I was a little relieved because that would make it easier to leave baseball behind. But that relief, if you could call it that, was short lived. Our third baseman struck out looking at a called third strike in the first inning and threw his bat in disgust at the umpire's call. My coach, an old war vet and Stanford graduate named John Herbold III, told him to stop pouting and take a seat. "If it's close enough to call a strike, you should be good enough to hit it" was his philosophy, and he had zero tolerance for blaming our mistakes on the umpire or anyone else. He sat down the third baseman and yelled to me, "Marty, go to third and take his spot." I ran into the game, and the first pitch was hit to me. I fielded it cleanly and made the play, which calmed my nerves. When I came up to bat the first time, I hit a hard line drive to the shortstop. This induced some praise from my coach, who yelled to the rest of the team, "He's a freshman, and he can hit. Some of you stinkin' seniors need to take some notes." The rest of the day was great. I got hits in my next two at-bats, and I stole three bases. I never left the lineup for the rest of the year.

I began to concentrate a lot on baseball again—probably too much. During this time I was reading in my Book of Mormon one evening. Some bad things were going on in the other room, and I went into my bedroom to escape it. As I read the Book of Mormon, I felt something that I had never felt so dramatically before. I felt calm, at home, strengthened, and peaceful. I knelt down, thanked Heavenly Father for that feeling, and asked if I could continue to feel it. As I was praying, I heard someone walk into the room. I knelt next to my bed and wondered if I would be made fun of. I was still on my knees, but I had stopped praying and started to plan a speech in my head about respecting my beliefs. After waiting a few minutes in vain for someone to make fun of me, I said another little prayer of thanks and sat up on my bed. It turned out that I had underestimated my roommate's level of respect for sacred things. He was standing in my doorway watching me the whole time. He said, "Hey, if I leave, will you say one of those for me?" I told him that he could pray for himself. He said, "My life is messed up right now. You are a good guy. God will listen to you. Please, say a prayer for me." I agreed to do so. He came back in a few minutes and made sure I had done so, and we talked on the bed about his life until late into the night.

This had a profound effect on me. It was my first missionary experience. Also, I looked up to this person a lot. He was a good baseball player who had been drafted straight out of high school but chose to forgo the minor leagues to play college ball and get an education. He was a ladies' man and was well liked by all who knew him. He had a great heart, and, even though he did not share my same beliefs, he had a sincerity about him. He had everything that I was working for, yet there he was, sitting on my bed and asking me about how his life could be better. I realized that day how fortunate I was to know what I know. From that day on, he made it so much easier for me to live how I wanted to live. The enticements to do bad things ceased after that experience. I was able to read my Book of Mormon on road trips without being bothered. I gained respect from my teammates. One day while in Northern California playing Stanford and University of San Francisco, we went over the Golden Gate Bridge as a team to a lookout point where you could see the San Francisco skyline. On the way back over, two of my friends on the team called me to the back of the bus. One of them said, "Hey, you are a good Mormon." I said, "Thank you. You are a good baseball player."

He continued, "We both have friends who are Mormon, and those who live it leave on missions when they are nineteen. Are you going to keep living it?" This was an interesting question. I was beginning to be tempted not to serve a mission because of the success I was having on the baseball field and the attention I was getting from some scouts. As I sat there on the bus, I kept thinking, "I have to serve a mission. It is what God wants me to do. I will never go wrong doing what he wants me to do. He will take care of me." I told my teammate that I was going to serve a mission. This is the moment when I felt like my decision was solidified. I never remember questioning again whether or not I would serve a mission.

When the day came to tell my coach I was leaving on a mission, I was very nervous. He was a grumpy old man at times and had even been known to throw things at his players on occasion. I also was afraid of offending him. He is now in the College Coaches Hall of Fame, and he had a lot of pull in the baseball world. He was a good man to have on your side if you wanted to play professional baseball, which I did. I was fasting that morning and prayed for strength. A number of my team-mates went with me to tell my coach. I walked into his office and said, "Coach, I am a member of The Church of Jesus Christ of Latter-day Saints, and—" He interrupted and finished my sentence, "You are going on a mission." I said, "Yes." "Water my plant," he said, as he handed me a plant and an old coke can and pointed to the door. My teammates were leaning up against the door trying to hear the coach's reaction. You should have seen the look on their faces when I walked out with a plant in my hand. I watered the plant and went back in to see my coach. He said, "Well, there are very few things in this life more important than baseball, and God might be one of them." I said, "To me he is, Coach." We parted ways on friendly terms. He even wrote me a few letters on my mission and would read my letters back to him to the team before games.

Everything that I have in my life right now I can connect to that opportunity I had to serve a mission. I am grateful I chose to put first things first in this situation. I know that he will take care of you if you put him before sports in your life your life as well.

Integrity before Sports

Elder Jospeh B. Wirthlin, former member of the Quorum of the Twelve Apostles, spoke of an experience from his days as a high school football player. He was playing in the Rocky Mountain Conference Championship game and had received a hand off and plunged into the line. On the bottom of the pile, he realized that he was just inches from the goal line. He shared the following concerning that experience:

> At that moment I was tempted to push the ball forward. I could have done it. And when the refs finally pulled the players off the pile, I would have been a hero. No one would have ever known. I had dreamed of this moment from the time I was a boy. And it was right there within my reach. But then I remembered the words of my mother. "Joseph," she had often said to me, "do what is right, no matter the consequence. Do what is right and things will turn out okay."
>
> I wanted so desperately to score that touchdown. But more than being a hero in the eyes of my friends, I wanted to be a hero in the eyes of my mother. And so I left the ball where it was—two inches from the goal line. I didn't know it at the time, but this was a defining experience. Had I moved the ball, I could have been a champion for a moment, but the reward of temporary glory would have carried with it too steep and too lasting a price. It would have engraved upon my conscience a scar that would have stayed with me the remainder of my life. I knew I must do what is right. (Joseph B. Wirthlin, "Life's Lessons Learned," *Ensign*, May 2007)

What would you have done? Would you have pushed the ball forward? If so, then you have made sports too high of a priority in your life. You have put winning ahead of honesty and integrity. You must put first things first.

School before Sports

We have touched on this throughout the book, but it is very important to put school ahead of sports. It is okay to dream big, but the truth of the matter is that the high majority of you who are reading this book will not make a living playing sports. We are not crushing dreams here, we had those dreams too and we pursued them as long as there was an opportunity to do so. You have to prepare your minds and hands to provide for and raise a family and that means putting school and learning first in your life. It doesn't not mean that you do not dedicate a lot of time to sports, but it may mean less video games, TV, hanging out, and so forth. You may need to sacrifice some of these things in order to excel at both school and sports.

Speaking to the youth of the Church, President Gordon B. Hinckley said,

> You are moving into the most competitive age the world has ever known. All around you is competition. You need all the education you can get. Sacrifice a car; sacrifice anything that is needed to be sacrificed to qualify yourselves to do the work of the world. That world will in large measure pay you what it thinks you are worth, and your worth will increase as you gain education and proficiency in your chosen field.
>
> You belong to a church that teaches the importance of education. You have a mandate from the Lord to educate your minds and your hearts and your hands. (Gordon B. Hinckley, "A Prophet's Counsel and Prayer for Youth," *Ensign*, Jan. 2001)

Both of us have a similar story when it comes to this principle. Our GPAs increased dramatically after we returned from our missions. What happened on our missions? Well, a couple of things. First, as Dustin's story in the "Do the Work" chapter highlighted, we learned to work. We learned that we could take the same effort we put forth in sports and apply it to something else. More important though, we had a shift in priorities; we started thinking about becoming husbands and fathers who would have to provide for a family. As we did so, we were able to move school up on the priority list and because of that, we were more successful in school. You could be a great student if you cared about being a great student as much as you did about being a great athlete. If you have not made this a priority in your life, you should begin to do so now.

Twenty-Second Time-Out

 Make a list of the top 10 activities that take up the most time in your life. Then rank them in order of which you are giving the highest priority to. Resist the temptation to write down the "right answers" here. Be brutally honest with yourself. We will use this list later.

1._____

2._____

3._____

4._____

5._____

6._____

7._____

8._____

9._____

10._____

Make Important Decisions Now

President Monson has often repeated the old adage, "When the time for decision arrives, the time for preparation is past" (Thomas S. Monson, "Dare To Stand Alone," *Ensign*, Nov. 2011). It is important that you decide now what your priorities are. Doing so will make it easier to make the decision and not get swayed by the moment when the time of decision comes.

What Does Putting Sports Ahead of Faith Look Like?

To those who have been critical of Coach Mendenhall and his football's fifth priority philosophy we would challenge to sit back and ask themselves, "Okay, what would it look like if football were put ahead of any of those things?"

What does it look like when young people put sports ahead of faith? As we have already talked about, they may miss Sunday meetings to play in a game or they may forgo a mission in order to play a sport. That is not putting first things first.

What does it look like when athletes put sports ahead of their family? They may be absent from a lot of family activities or miss significant family events in order to play a game. They may make their teammates a more significant part of their life than their siblings or parents. That would not be putting first things first.

What does it look like when athletes put sports ahead of knowledge and schooling? They may be spending hours practicing their sport but doing minimal effort in school. This is a very common phenomenon. When sports dreams began to fade into fantasy, as they do with most of us, your schooling and how you performed there will be so much more important than what you achieved in sports. If you were to put sports ahead of knowledge and schooling, you would not be putting first things first.

What does it look like when young people put sports above their friends? This one could be tricky. Of course they would not miss practice to hang out and do something with a friend that could be done later, but there may arise times when they would either put in some extra work or help out a friend who is really in need. It is important that sports do not become such a big part of life that they become self-centered and don't think of those around them. If you were to do so, you would not be putting first things first.

The fact is that there are many things in life more important than sports, and we need to make sure that we put first things first. The Lord will bless us in all areas of our life as we do so.

Twenty-Second Time-Out

 Analyze your life according to the list that you made in the previous twenty-second time-out. Are you putting first things first? If not what do you need to adjust? Reorder your priority list the way you think it should be ordered.

1._____

2._____

3._____

4._____

5._____

6._____

7._____

8._____

9._____

10._____

Off-the-Field Applications

You will have literally thousands of times throughout your life when you will have to decide to put first things first, and chapters can be written about those moments. But the fact is that no matter the season of life, the first step will be for you to decide what should be first priority in your life at that moment. What are your highest priorities right now? You should prayerfully ask this question now and often as you continue through life because life changes. God will direct you in this matter. Your life right now is relatively simple. You have harder questions regarding priorities in the future. But if you learn now to put first things first, it will be easier to do so in the future.

The "Do The Work" Challenge

Read over some of the notes you made while pondering the twenty-second time-outs from this chapter. Identify one or two SMART goals that will help you to put first things first

_____

_____

_____

_____

_____

_____

_____

_____

_____

_____

_____

_____

_____

_____

_____

_____

_____

_____

_____

_____

_____

_____

_____

_____

_____

_____

_____

_____

Chapter 5:

STRIVE TO BE YOUR BEST, NOT THE BEST

Pregame Pep Talk

> "There is no such thing as an overachiever. We are all under-achievers to different degrees. No one has ever achieved anything he or she wasn't capable of. Whatever you have accomplished you could have accomplished more. Whatever you have done, you could have done it better"
> **—John Wooden**

Those who will have the most success in sports are those who strive to become the best *they* can be. They do not become content even when they are on top because they do not view their accomplishments in relation to others. They strive for continual improvement. Hall of Fame basketball coach John Wooden once taught, "Don't measure yourself by what you have accomplished, but by what you should have accomplished with your ability." Some who excel at sports when they are young, due to God-given ability, never reach their full potential because they become content with being "*the* best" instead of "*their* best." This is a hard hurdle to over-come, and it can only be overcome in one way, and that is by living this principle.

The principle of being *your* best, not *the* best applies in other important ways too. There will be times when you are obviously not the best one on the field or court. Inevitably you will reach this moment. Sports are like a funnel. At the beginning it is not too remarkable to be the best kid on your city league team, but as you move up the ranks, more and more players become more and more normal until finally they are sifted out and don't get to move on to the next level. If your goal is to be the best, what happens when you realize that you are not the best anymore? Many who face this reality fade into oblivion. They get lazy and lax because it is easier for them to act like they are not trying than it is to try and not be the best.

One of the people that comes to mind when we think of being your best instead of the best is a teammate of ours named Dave. Dave desperately wanted to play college baseball. He got home from his mission and tried out but was cut. He worked from the moment he was cut until tryouts the next year. When cuts came around, he once again found himself without a spot on the team. Crushed, he approached the coach and told him that he would do anything. The coach told him that he could have a spot on the team as a manager. Dave agreed to do so as long as he was able to practice with the team and wear the uniform. Coach agreed, and Dave began to work. Though he was only a team manager, no one out worked Dave. His face would literally turn bright red as he ran sprints with us. Every swing he took he gave full effort. Something began to happen. Dave began to get better. He would invite teammates to meet him early in the morning and take batting practice before our first classes. Some wondered why this "team manager" was working so hard. Well, he was not a team manager for long. In fact, toward the end of the year Dave was getting some major playing time and significantly contributing to the team. The next year, he was a team captain. Dave is a great example of someone who was willing to do the work and strive to be *his* best even if he had no hope of being *the* best.

Imagine what would happen if those with exceptional talent learned to work to develop themselves like Dave did. This is why it is important to learn to do the work to become your best, not the best, even if you are the best. If you work to be the best, you place a ceiling on your development. If you can walk out on the track and outrun the person next to you, push the guy off of the line in front of you, dribble around the defender guarding you, or throw a fastball by the batter, you may stop working if your goal is to be the best. But in so doing, you would be robbing yourself.

We have already talked about Kobe Bryant in the "Do the Work" chapter but he is a good example of this principle as well. Kobe Bryant is a fourteen-time NBA All Star, NBA Most Valuable Player Award winner, and five-time NBA Champion. He is also a great example of one who strives to be *his* best even when he is considered by many to be *the* best. Here is an interview where Kobe speaks of constantly trying to improve.

Men's Fitness: How many shots do you shoot in a day?

Kobe: It's between 700 to 1,000 makes a day.

Men's Fitness: Do you have any training tips, aside from Olympic lifts, that you'd recommend to younger basketball players.

Kobe: The thing that I tell them all the time is consistency. If they watch me train, running on a track, it doesn't look like I'm over-exerting myself. It's a consistency with which you do it, in other words, it's an every-day-thing. You have a program, and a schedule, and you have to abide by that, religiously. You just stick to it, and it's the consistency that pays off.

Men's Fitness: If you could pinpoint one part of your game— and this would really be nitpicking—what would it be?

Kobe: It depends—I usually make those evaluations at the end of the season, along with Phil (Jackson) and the rest of the coaching staff, and break down the season and how I progress, and how I evolve as a player, go into the summer with a plan, exactly what I need to work on.

Men's Fitness: *So that's every summer? You break your game down?*

Kobe: *Oh yeah. You have to.*

(http://www.mensfitness.com/leisure/entertainment/kobe-bryant)

Can you see how it would be detrimental to Kobe Bryant if his goal was to be the best? He may have stopped working a long time ago. Whether you are the best or not, seeking to be the best may prevent you from becoming *your* best. Seeking to be your best is a liberating attitude. You are no longer threatened by the accomplishments of your teammates, no longer looking over your shoulder to see who is getting the attention. You are free to become your best self, to give all you can give, and to expect the same of your teammates, regardless of their talent level.

Shad's Experience

I have a major regret from high school. After my senior year of baseball, I was playing American Legion baseball. My best friend, Chris, had just been drafted by the Baltimore Oriels and had left for rookie ball. Chris was an incredible teammate of mine. We had played on each other's team for almost our whole life. We had won many championships together and were really close.

When he left, the local newspaper did an article on me. The article was entitled, "From the Shadows, Martin's Bat Emerges." The writer who interviewed me started the article this way:

"By now, Shad Martin is used to walking in the shadows. For three years Martin was the Falcon's starting shortstop. In two of those years, the Falcons were the Golden League champions. He batted over .350 in his high school career, and was deemed Palmdale's "most offensive" player after this past season. Still, Martin always played second-fiddle to the Falcons all league catcher, Chris, who was a late-round draft pick of the Baltimore Oriels in the Major League draft in June. Chris also happened to be his best friend.

"My whole high school career, I played in Chris's shadow. In high school he always had the upper-hand. Competing with him made both of us a lot better."

He then went on to say, "But during the recently completed American Legion season, everyone was in Martin's shadow as he hit an even .500 with two homers, 17 RBI's and a slugging percentage of .798".

What bugged me so badly about what appeared to be a very complimentary article even almost twenty years later as I look back? Somehow I let a reporter view my accomplishments in relation to my teammates, even one of my best friends. I talked to Chris on the phone the day the article came out and told him I was sorry. I could tell he was kind of bugged. I wish I could go back and redo the interview now that I understand the importance of being my best and not the best. I would have said it this way:

"I loved playing with Chris. We were not in competition with each other. We were teammates working together to win championships. I did my best and he did his best and together we have won many games and championships. He is my friend and I am better for having played with such a great player."

Such an answer would have shown that I did not view my accomplishments in relations to others; unfortunately at that time, I probably did. It would have shown that I was striving to be my best instead of the best. Unfortunately in this case, and in some others I am sure, my desire to be the best hurt a friend and revealed my selfishness. This mistake helped me learn a lesson I remembered and never repeated.

This was a very timely lesson as well. A few months later I would begin my college baseball career. When I arrived on campus, I realized that I was a boy among men. Everyone was faster, stronger, and better than I was. I remember one occasion when we were waiting on a bus before we were to play Stanford. My Hall of Fame coach began to go up and down the aisle of the bus and tell each of us what he thought of us. He told some to stop drinking beer, some to hit the weights, and some he showered with compliments. I felt so insignificant at the time that I wondered if he would just skip me. When he came to me he said, "Martin, you can't hit, you can't throw, you can't run, but you might be the one here that makes it to the show, why? Because you work and you don't drink beer. That is the only reason why you are starting right now. You work and you don't drink beer." I remember feeling complimented and put down at the same time. If I would have been worried about being the best I may have stopped working and given up. Instead I just worked to be my best.

As I did so, something began to happen. I began to discover strengths that were not apparent in my high school days. I became the second hitter. The leadoff hitter ended up playing professional baseball and the third hitter played major league baseball for the Baltimore Orioles. Because of this I was asked to sacrifice bunt a lot and to purposely hit harmless ground balls to the right side of the infield to move the runner to first base. That was not the most glorious job, but I took it seriously and worked hard at it. By the end of the year, I had the single season school record for sacrifice bunts in a season, which still stands today, and when I left on my mission my coach said in the paper that I was the best number two hitter he had ever coached. I had never batted second in high school and I had no idea that I even had those strengths. That year my coach helped me see what my strengths were. I realized that my best was different than my teammate's best. We were good in different ways. I was not worried about being in their shadow, I was just worried about being my best.

Seek Vertical Instead of Horizontal Praise

One of the concepts that we would like to emphasize here is the concept of vertical praise. John Wooden once said, "Be more concerned with your character than your reputation, because your character is what you really are, while your reputation is merely what others think you are." On another occasion he said, "You can't let praise or criticism get to you. It's a weakness to get caught up in either one." These two quotes lead nicely into what we mean by vertical praise. Vertical praise means that you keep your eyes up to get your feedback from above, not from those around you. There are only two people in the universe that know how you are performing in relation to the talents and gifts that have been given to you: you and God. Sometimes coaches will misjudge this. They will think you are being lazy when you are tired or they will think you are giving your all because of the success you are having, when in reality you have so much more to give. Fans may criticize you and say you are dogging it or not giving your best when you really are, or they may praise you when you are not giving your best because your mediocre effort is good enough to make you look good. You can see that looking for horizontal praise or criticism can limit your progression.

Vertical praise is different. It is looking into your own heart and, most important, looking to God who knows everything for feedback. He knows when you are faking an injury to get out of work, he knows when you are giving your all, and he sees things as they really are. He also cares about all of the right things. Results are secondary to Him. In the parable of the talents you will notice that the person who was entrusted with two talents and got two more and was rewarded and received the same commendation as the one who was entrusted with five and worked to get five more: "Well done, thou good and faithful servant: thou hast been faithful over a few things, I will make thee ruler over many things" (Matthew 25:21–23). You can't always control what others think of you, but God is constant and you can count on the fact that he is pleased when you give an honest effort. Vertical praise helps you reach your full potential, horizontal praise can be very debilitating when it is your main source of feedback. As we mentioned before, we like to call this attitude having an "eyes up" attitude. There is power in looking to God.

In Matthew 14, we read the account of Jesus walking on water. His disciples were afraid and unsure if it was really Jesus. One of the disciples, Peter, asks the Savior if he might be allowed to walk to him on the water. Jesus allowed him to do so and Peter actually walked on water! His eyes were focused on Jesus as he approached him, but then something very interesting happened. Peter lost focus. He began to see all of the things around him that should have been preventing him from walking on water; he doubted and in doing so began to sink.

We pause here to make a point before moving on to the rest of the story. Do we as individuals and do you as an athlete understand how truly great you can become if you have an "eyes up" attitude and look to Jesus Christ to assist you? Do you trust that he knows what is best for you and how to help you become your very best self both as a person and as an athlete? Peter was doing something much more impressive than he or his fellow fisherman friends ever thought he was capable of doing when he trusted and focused on Jesus. However, when he allowed doubt to set in, and when he lost focus on the only person who could truly help him be his best, he began to sink. The message is that in order for you to become your very best and to accomplish things that you never could accomplish otherwise, you need to look vertically to God, not horizontally to those around you.

President Howard W. Hunter taught the following concerning this story,

> While [Peter's] eyes were fixed on the Lord, the wind might toss his hair, and the spray might drench his robes, but all was well' [Frederic W. Farrar, *The Life of Christ* (1964), 311]. Only when with wavering faith he removed his glance from the Master to look at the furious waves and the black gulf beneath him, only then did he begin to sink. . . .
>
> It is my firm belief that if as individual people . . . we could, like Peter, fix our eyes on Jesus, we too might walk triumphantly over the "swelling waves" . . . But if we turn away our eyes from him in whom we must believe, as it is so easy to do . . . , if we look to the power and fury of those terrible and destructive elements around us rather than to him who can help and save us, then we shall inevitably sink in a sea of conflict sorrow and despair. (Howard W. Hunter, *"The Beacon in the Harbor of Peace," Ensign* Nov. 1992, 19)

Keeping your "eyes up" means that you ask for help from your Father in heaven. It means that you trust in him. No matter what the situation, good or bad, trust that he knows what he is doing and that he knows what you are capable of doing and becoming as an athlete and as a person. Just as you must learn to keep your "eye on the ball" to be successful in sports, you must keep your eye on the Savior to be successful as a person and trust that He will help you to be your very best at whatever you are seeking to excel in.

Now, continuing with the rest of this great story in Matthew. What happened to Peter? Did he sink to the bottom of sea? In verse 30 we read that Peter looked back at Jesus and said, "Lord, save me!" And then in 31: "And immediately Jesus stretched forth his hand and caught him, and said unto him, O thou of little faith, wherefore didst thou doubt?" He immediately caught him and helped him! He immediately was there to love him and then to teach him the reason he did not finish his goal of walking to Jesus. In your efforts to be the best athlete you can be and to be the best person you can become, remember that with the help of the Savior, you can become so much more, but you must ask him for help to become your best or to do something great, and then you must listen to his advice on how to do that and the stay focused on him. You will still fail as an athlete sometimes. That is part of sports and actually one of the great lessons we can learn from them, but if you learn look to God and keep your "eyes up," you will never fail as an individual. When you need help, remember to call out to him for help and that he, just as he did with Peter, will immediately stretch forth his hand and catch you.

Twenty-Second Time-Out

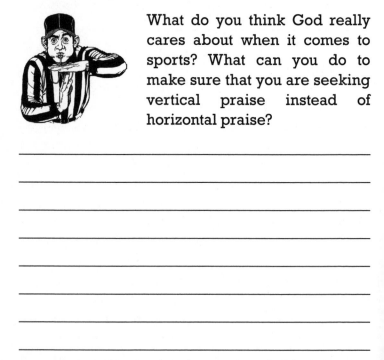

What do you think God really cares about when it comes to sports? What can you do to make sure that you are seeking vertical praise instead of horizontal praise?

_____

_____

_____

_____

_____

_____

_____

_____

_____

_____

_____

Concentrate on What *You* Have Control of When Becoming Your Best Self

There is an application of this principle that mingles well with the "do the work" principle discussed earlier. There are some things outside of your control when you play sports, and it really does not do much good to spend your time and energy on such things. For example, you may feel that a teammate is starting over you because his father is a big donor to the booster club or because his dad is the coach or whatever reason. The fact is that sometimes this is true. So what are you going to do about it? You have no control over it, and spending precious energy worrying about such things keeps you from becoming your best self. Someone may stop you from playing, but they can't stop you from working to be your best.

There was a young man in Southern California that was so much better than the young man who backed him up at catcher on the baseball team. In spite of this the coach of their team had him split time with another young man. Why? The coach did not like members of the LDS church. The backup catcher was a young man that went to the coach's church. What was the LDS catcher supposed to do? He could have pouted and given up. Instead of pouting or quitting, this young man started working. He hit the weights and increased his strength and spent a lot of time working at catching and hitting. Eventually he ended up playing college baseball.

Working to become your best is something that is always within your control. No one can stop you from doing it. Have you ever heard of a coach stopping a player from working? You can run harder, lift harder, concentrate harder, and simply "do the work." If you are worried about becoming *your* best self, you will work in any situation. If you are worried about being *the* best, you will become discouraged and maybe even give up.

Listen to the Coach and Be Teachable

One of the dangers of seeking to be the best instead of your best is that you worry too much about *looking* good and not enough about *being* good. Someone who wants to become their best hungers and thirsts for ways to become better. They are excited for any opportunity to improve and they view the coaching they receive as an opportunity to do so.

Some are not interested in coaching. When someone is teaching them, it is like one can see them saying in their head, "Okay, okay. Be quiet; I know what I'm doing." Or they get a case of the "Yeah, buts." You know what those are. If not, here are some examples:

Coach: You need to be more aggressive on defense.
Uncoachable Player: Yeah, but I don't want to get in foul trouble.

Coach: You need to look off the safety before you throw that pass.
Uncoachable player: Yeah, but the line isn't giving me enough time to do so.

You get the idea. One of the problems with our society is that we spend so much time formulating excuses and not enough time seeking real improvement and formulating solutions. Being teachable is part of being your best self.

Twenty-Second Time-Out

Do you have a case of the "Yeah, buts"? What can you do or stop doing to become more coachable?

_____

_____

_____

_____

_____

_____

_____

_____

_____

_____

Off-the-Field Applications

It is not hard to see the Off-the-Field Applications when it comes to being your best instead of the best. But here are some that came to our minds. If you are called on a mission and are seeking horizontal praise, you may be disappointed. Some don't baptize or even teach a lot of people on their missions. Others baptize many people. This is often more of a function of where you serve rather than how. God knows if you are doing all you can, and he will reward you. Learning to seek vertical praise will bless you to feel good about your service, regardless of noticeable outcomes. You can have confidence that God is pleased with your service even if your service does not seem so impressive to others. You will be pleased with yourself and have a quiet confidence that you have worked to become the best missionary that you could be.

Young women may choose to forgo some of the things in life that would bring more worldly or horizontal praise to be a mother. You would do well to learn the lesson of seeking vertical praise now. For those who are able, becoming a mother is one of the most noble and Christlike things that can be done on this earth. Ask any mother though, and they will tell you that it does not come with many "horizontal" rewards. Some in the world today will even see you with a large family or a young family and act as though you are irresponsible and feel sorry for you. In such situations, learning to seek vertical praise, which is sure to come from your Father in Heaven, would be a great blessing to have.

One of the other main applications here is being humble and teachable. We knew two young men who went on missions. One began by telling his trainer, "You will not mess with me." He resisted any feedback he received from his trainer and considered it a put down. In fact, when his trainer told him to tuck his pants into his sock before his first bike ride, the new missionary refused to do so. The trainer was doing this so that his pants would not get caught in his bike chain, but the new missionary was so unteachable he would not even listen to this simple advice. A mile down the road, his brand-new suit was ripped from the bottom of the pant leg to above his knee. He struggled his whole mission.

The second missionary said on the first day of his mission, "I prayed for a good trainer. I am going to trust you and do whatever you ask me to do. I just want to be the best missionary I can be." He had an incredible mission.

Learn to learn from others now. It will serve you well the

rest of your life. No matter what your profession or path in life, you will progress so much quicker if you learn to receive and implement feedback from those who care enough to give it. We know one individual in charge of hiring for a large organization. He said that humility and teachability is non-negotiable in his organization. If someone lacked that trait, they would not be hired because they would never become what another, less talented person who was willing to be tutored, would become. If you have a case of the "Yeah, buts," you need to get rid of it because it is an easily recognizable condition that will be debilitating to you in almost every aspect of your life if you do not work on it now. Sports give you a chance to overcome the "Yeah, buts" and to learn to take responsibility.

Seeking to be your best instead of the best allows you to truly progress. You become independent of any other person's opinion including coaches, teammates, or fans. At the same time you become teachable so you are interested in feedback but not discouraged or pacified by it.

The "Do The Work" Challenge

Read over some of the notes you made while pondering the twenty-second time-outs from this chapter. Identify one or two SMART goals that will help you become your best.

_____

_____

_____

_____

_____

_____

_____

_____

_____

_____

_____

_____

_____

_____

_____

_____

_____

_____

_____

_____

_____

_____

_____

_____

_____

_____

_____

CONCLUSION

We hope that the principles in this book will be a blessing to you and help you reach your full potential as an athlete and that you will be able to take those lessons from the field or court and apply them into your life. After reading this book, we hope you can sign this creed we developed especially for athletes. Signing this creed means that you commit to do the work you have written down at the end of each a chapter. These principles will bless anyone who lives them, but they were created especially for athletes.

A Creed Especially for Athletes

I'll "do the work." I will not let defeat, fatigue, or laziness stop me from becoming all that I was intended to become. I have Monday through Sunday to "do the work," I will not plan on "doing the work" someday. Someday is where my goals go to die. I understand that work means sacrifice and I am willing to make sacrifices to be great.

I will compete without contempt. I will not roll over and give up, but when I knock someone down I will help them up. I will appreciate the greatness of my opponents and respect them. I will not seek to embarrass, demean, or hurt an opponent, and if I sense that I have done so, I will make it right.

I will seek to bless and not impress. I will use the "sportlight" that shines on me to lift others. When others see me play, they will see that I do not check my faith at the door. I will use the gifts God blessed me with to do as much good as possible and to be a friend to the friendless, a protection to the weak, and a light to those who are in darkness.

I will put first things first. My faith, my family, my friends, or my education will never be sacrifices on the altar of sports. I want to win but I will win the right way. I would rather lose fair than win cheap.

I will seek to be my best. If I end up being the best that is fine, but I will not be pacified into contentment by the praise of others or discouraged by their doubts in me and my abilities. I will not view my accomplishments in relation to others but will view it as an accomplishment when I reach my full potential. I will not view others' successes as my failures. I will care more about vertical feedback than horizontal.

In short, I will keep my eyes up and do the work.

X

Thank you for signing this creed. Our goal is to create a culture of young athletes that live by these very important principles. We would like to connect you with other athletes who have taken this creed. We encourage you to visit www .especiallyforathletes.com to learn of upcoming events associated with this book and to share the experiences you have as you "do the work" to apply these principles. We know that you will have incredible experiences to share and that those experiences will give others courage to do the same. God bless you for using your "sportlight" to make a difference.

ACKNOWLEDGMENTS

I would like to dedicate this book to the greatest coach I ever had, which happened to be my father. He used sports to teach me so many lessons many of which I have passed on in this book. I dedicate this book to the greatest fan I ever had, which happened to be my mother. I can still see her sitting under that umbrella in the desert sun. She never missed a game. I dedicate this book to the greatest opponent I ever had, which happened to be my childhood friend and teammate Chris Paxton. No level of competition I ever reached compared to our driveway basketball and baseball games.

I would also like to dedicate this book to my brothers Shane, Shawn and Sheldon who were always and will always be my best friends. I dedicate this book to my coaches and teammates who taught me these lessons. I also want to dedicate this book to everyone who realizes that sports can be so much more than just a game and who use their gifts to lift.

I thank my wife, the most incredible women I have ever met, and my children who allow me to do what I am passionate about and who render unyielding support to me.

I also want to thank Dustin. He is one of those people who are inspiring to be around. Writing this book with him has made me a better person and my hope is that his words in this book bless others lives as much as they have mine.

—Shad Martin

I would like to dedicate this book to all those willing to risk failure, in whatever endeavor, for the shot at being great at something, and to those many athletes I have been blessed to coach and will coach in the future. This message is for you.

I wish to thank to my parents Wade and Shelley for teaching me how to work, my brothers Ryan and Nate for teaching me how to compete, and to my sister Maegan for her patience.

I also wish to thank my many teammates and coaches over the years. Thank you Shad for the great blessing it has been to write this book with you. Shad is a gifted teacher and leader, and a friend every person should have the chance to have.

To my beautiful wife and best friend Jamie, the page is too small, but thank you for listening and for smiling.

Finally, to all those who love their hobbies, their professions, and their talents enough to give to others in order to help lift another, the world needs more of you. Thank you for keeping your eyes up to God and for not waiting for "someday" to do the work.

—Dustin Smith

ABOUT THE AUTHORS

Shad Martin has taught semi-nary for ten years and has spoken at youth conferences, EFY's, BYU Education Week, and at sports camps all over the country. He also recently published his first book, *Ten Scriptures to Get You Through High School*. Sports have been a major part of Shad's life. As a high school athlete, Shad was an all-league performer in both basketball and baseball at Palmdale High school  in Palmdale, California. After high school, Shad attended California State University at Los Angeles on a baseball scholarship where he started and played second base as a freshman. He left his scholar-ship to serve a two-year mission in Harrisburg, Pennsylvania, and then decided to attend and play baseball at Ricks College in Idaho. After graduating from Ricks College, Shad attended Brigham Young University where he graduated with a degree in economics. He then completed a masters degree at Utah State University. Shad is married to Robin Creer and has three daughters. He loves the Church and the Prophet and considers having the opportunity to teach and interact with the youth of the Church one of his greatest blessings.

 **D**ustin Smith has taken his expe-rience as an athlete, a coach, an organizer of programs for the devel-opment of thousands of athletes, and from speaking to youth groups around the country over the last decade, and shared what he believes to be a fun-damental message all athletes would be made better by understanding and applying. His central message of "doing the work" with an "eyes up" approach

is a message not only valuable to the aspiring young athlete, but a message applicable in attacking all the challenges that life presents. A public speaker, coach, business owner and father of six children, Dustin and his wife Jamie live in Cedar Hills, Utah.